Contents

Workbook 11

Getting the Right People to do the Right Job

Institute of Management Programme

the Institute
of Management
FOUNDATION

Pergamon
Open
Learning

Pergamon Open Learning

An imprint of Butterworth-Heinemann

Linacre House, Jordan Hill, Oxford OX2 8DP

A division of Reed Educational and Professional Publishing Ltd

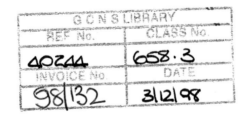 A member of the Reed Elsevier plc group

OXFORD BOSTON JOHANNESBURG

MELBOURNE NEW DELHI SINGAPORE

First published 1997

British Library Cataloguing in Publication Data
A catalogue record for this book is available from the British Library

ISBN 0 7506 3660 2

Typeset by Avocet Typeset, Brill, Aylesbury, Bucks
Printed and bound in Great Britain

Series overview

The Institute of Management Open Learning Programme is a series of workbooks prepared by the Institute of Management and Pergamon Open Learning for managers seeking to develop themselves.

Comprising seventeen open learning workbooks, the programme covers the best of modern management theory and practice, and each workbook provides a range of frameworks and techniques to improve your effectiveness as a manager, thus helping you acquire the knowledge and skill to make you fully competent in your role.

Each workbook is written by an experienced management writer and covers an important management topic or theme. The activities both reinforce learning and help to relate the generic ideas to your individual work context. While coverage of each topic is fully comprehensive, additional reading suggestions and reference sources are given for those who wish to study to a greater depth.

Designed to be practical, stimulating and challenging, the aim of the workbooks is to improve performance at work by benefiting you and your organization. This practical focus is at the heart of the competence based approach that has been adopted by the programme.

The structure of the programme

The design and overall structure of the programme has two main organizing principles, both of which are closely linked to the national standards for management developed by the MCI (Management Charter Initiative).

First, the workbooks are grouped according to the key roles of management.

- Underpinning the management standards are a series of **personal competences** which describe the personal skills required by all managers, which are essential to skill in all the main functional or key role areas.
- **Manage Activities** describes the principles of managing processes and activities, with service to the customer as an essential part of this.
- **Manage Resources** describes the acquisition, control and monitoring of financial and other resources.
- **Manage People** looks at the key skills involved in leadership, developing one's staff and managing their performance.

■ **Manage Information** discusses the acquisition, storage and use of information for communication, problem solving and decision making.

In addition, there are three specialized key roles: **Manage Quality, Manage Projects** and **Manage Energy**. The workbooks cover the first two of these. Unlike the four primary key roles above, these are not compulsory for certificate, diploma or S/NVQ requirements, but provide options for the latter.

Together, these key roles provide a comprehensive description of the fundamental principles of management as it applies in any organization – commercial, maintained sector or not-for-profit.

Second, the programme is organized according to **levels of management**, seniority and responsibility.

Level 4 represents first line management. In accredited programmes this is equivalent to S/NVQ Level 4, Certificate in Management or CMS. Level 5 is equivalent to middle/senior management and is accredited at S/NVQ Level 5, Diploma in Management or DMS. There are two S/NVQs at Level 5: Operational Management and Strategic Management. The operations role is focussed internally within an organization on the maintenance of systems and standards of output, whilst the strategic role is focussed on the whole organization, including the external operating environment, and looks at setting directions.

Together, the workbooks cover all the background knowledge you need to have for all units of competence in the MCI standards at Level 4 and Level 5 (apart from the specialized units in the key role Manage Energy). They also provide skills development and opportunities for portfolio building.

For a comprehensive list of workbooks, see page ix. For a comprehensive list of links with the standards, see the *User Guide.*

How to use the programme

The programme is deliberately designed to be flexible and can be used in a variety of ways:

■ to update on important management topics and themes, or develop individual skills: as the workbooks are grouped according to themes, it should be easy for you to pick out one that suits your needs

■ as part of generic management development programmes: you can choose the modules that fit the themes of the programme

■ as part of, and in support of, accredited competence-based programmes.

For N/SVQs at both Levels 4 and 5, there are options in the combinations of units that make up the various awards. By using the map provided in the *User Guide*, individuals will be able to select the workbooks appropriate to their specific needs, and their chosen accreditation options. Some of the activities will help you provide evidence for your portfolio; where we think this is the case, we give the relevant reference to the standards.

For Certificate or CMS, Diploma or DMS, individuals should choose modules that not only meet their individual needs but also satisfy the requirements of the delivering body and the awarding body.

You may need help and guidance in these choices, and the *User Guide* sets out the options and advice in much more detail. A fuller description of the potential uses of this material in evidence gathering and portfolio building can also be found in the *User Guide*, as can a detailed description of the contents of each workbook.

Workbooks in the Institute of Management Open Learning Programme

Personal Competences (Levels 4 and 5)

  1 *The Influential Manager**
  2 *Managing Yourself**

Manage Activities (Level 4)

  3 *Understanding Business Process Management*
  4 *Customer Focus*

Manage Activities (Level 5)

  5 *Getting TQM to Work*
  6 *Leading from the Front*
  7 *Improving Your Organization's Success*

Manage Resources (Level 4)

  8 *Project Management*
  9 *Budgeting and Financial Control*

Manage Resources (Level 5)

10 *Effective Financial and Resource Management*

Manage People (Level 4)

  1 *The Influential Manager*
  2 *Managing Yourself*
11 *Getting the Right People to do the Right Job*
12 *Developing Yourself and Your Staff*
13 *Building a High Performance Team*

Manage People (Level 5)

14 *The New Model Leader*

Manage Information (Level 4)

15 *Making Rational Decisions*
16 *Communication*

Manage Information (Level 5)

17 *Successful Information Management*

Manage Quality (Level 4)

3 *Understanding Business Process Management**
4 *Customer Focus**

Manage Quality (Level 5)

5 *Getting TQM to Work**

Manage Projects (Level 4)

8 *Project Management**

Manage Projects (Level 5)

8 *Project Management**

Support Materials

18 *User Guide*
19 *Mentor Guide*

An asterisk indicates that a particular workbook also contains material suitable for a particular key role or personal competence.

Links to qualifications

S/NVQ programmes

This workbook can help candidates to achieve credit and develop skills in the key role Manage People and covers the following units and elements:

C8   Select personnel for activities
C8.1   Identify personnel requirements
C8.2   Select required personnel
C15   Respond to poor performance in your team
C15.1   Help team members who have problems affecting their performance
C15.2   Contribute to implementing disciplinary and grievance procedures
C16   Deal with poor performance in your team
C16.1   Support team members who have problems affecting their performance
C16.2   Implement disciplinary and grievance procedures
C16.3   Dismiss team members whose performance is unsatisfactory
C17   Redeploy personnel and make redundancies
C17.1   Plan the redeployment of personnel
C17.2   Redeploy personnel
C17.3   Make personnel redundant

In addition, it covers the following elements from the key role Manage Activities:

A2.2   Maintain a healthy, safe and productive work environment
A3.3   Maintain a healthy, safe and productive work environment

Certificate and Diploma programmes

This workbook, together with the other workbooks on managing people (1 – *The Influential Manager*, 2 – *Managing Yourself*, 12 – *Developing Yourself and Your Staff* and 13 – *Building a High Performance Team*) covers all of the knowledge required in the key role Manage People for Certificate in Management and CMS programmes.

Links to other workbooks

The other workbooks in the key role Manage People at Level 4 are:

12 *Developing Yourself and Your Staff*
13 *Building a High Performance Team*

and at Level 5:

14 *The New Model Leader*

The theme of this workbook is closely associated with:

16 *Communication*

Introduction

Most organizations, over recent years, have come to the realization that their **people** are their most important and valuable resource. Companies now accept that, ultimately, all the plans, systems, processes and procedures become worthless and irrelevant unless **people** can bring them to life and make them work.

In this workbook, *Getting the Right People to do the Right Job*, we will be looking at how you can thread a safe path through the tricky minefields of recruitment and selection (getting the right people), and the even more complex – and potentially dangerous – areas of grievance and disciplinary procedures and other related personnel issues involved in building an effective working environment (doing the job right).

We'll also be focusing on the manager's role as a workplace counsellor and how you can work with staff to help them to explore the issues which may be affecting their work performance.

Health and safety in the workplace is a key management issue and we will be looking at the current legislation which you, as a manager, need to be aware of.

The final section of this workbook focuses on the legal aspects of personnel management, including Health and Safety.

This workbook, then, covers what are traditionally called personnel issues. These are those responsibilities we have as employers of people in organizations.

They range from the procedural (recruitment and discipline) through the people oriented (like counselling) to the environmental (Health and Safety), and they are bounded by legislation and accepted good practice.

Among the purposes of this workbook are to set out the legislative requirements and the elements of good practice which managers in all organizations should know.

Objectives

By the end of this workbook you should be able to:

- Apply techniques for recruitment and selection of staff
- Implement disciplinary procedures and dismiss staff
- Carry out grievance procedures fairly and objectively

- Conform to the redundancy procedures stipulated by both your organization and the law
- Counsel staff who are not meeting required work standards
- Understand the legal requirements of personnel management, including recruitment, dismissal and health and safety of staff

Section 1 Recruiting and selecting the right people

Introduction

Human resource planning, deciding how many people you will need to do which jobs, is the first step in the management of the recruitment process. The second step is actually finding the right people to do those jobs. As a manager, you will no doubt from time to time be charged with the task of recruiting and appointing a new member of staff. This is a complex challenge which requires you to look in the right place to find a selection of people from which to make your choice. Actually choosing involves asking the right kinds of questions to find out what you need to know and then judging which person will best be able to do the job **and** fit in with the existing team. The wrong choice is likely to bring you many sleepless nights and stress-filled working days.

In this section we will be looking at some of the techniques you can use to undertake human resource planning, and to ensure that, wherever possible, you make wise recruitment choices that benefit your organization, your team and yourself. Good recruitment procedures not only ensure that your approach is rational and help to secure good staff, but also help to ensure that your approach is fair and complies with the requirements of the law.

Human resource planning

Clearly, there will be occasions when key staff leave your organization and those vacancies need to be filled. But the wise manager also needs to take a longer term view and look at possible requirements for staff in the future.

ACTIVITY 1

List two techniques you know of to identify the number and type of staff you might need to recruit for your organization one year from now:

1

2

Are these techniques appropriate?

FEEDBACK

The four main approaches to medium and long-term human resource planning are:

- **managerial judgement**
  Managers predict, using their knowledge, expertise and experience, likely future staffing requirements. The advantage of this technique is that people with an in-depth understanding of the business are usually able to do well when asked to forecast future trends. The disadvantage is that human error can sometimes result in costly mistakes.

- **statistical analysis**
  Specialists (often assisted by managerial judgement) use a range of techniques – from simple extrapolation through to regression and correlation studies and econometric models. These techniques are based on the notion that past trends are likely to continue in the future. The main disadvantage is that statistics are less sensitive to changes in organizational or environmental changes.

- **work study**
  Work study exercises (although falling out of favour with many organizations) can be useful to establish the precise number of person hours needed per unit of output. Human resource predictions can be made on the basis of this information, as long as wastage and absenteeism is taken into account, and the figures are regularly and rigorously monitored and revised.

- **productivity measurement**
  This technique (which is similar to work study) focuses on output targets. Once output targets are identified, these figures are divided by the anticipated productivity rates. The resulting figures will give an indication of the number of staff needed. Productivity measurement is useful if (a) both outputs and inputs are easily quantifiable and (b) account is taken of the impact of planned technological change on employee productivity.

Most organizations use a combination of these methods to identify their human resource requirements for the future, but also take into account how organizational changes may affect the number of people needed. These changes might include, for example:

- job rotation
- job sharing
- introduction of multi-skilled work groups

Other factors must also be taken into consideration, such as trends in people leaving the organization. On closer examination, it could be that leavers are, for instance:

- mostly people between the ages of 19 and 24
- mostly people from the chemical processing department
- mostly people involved in clerical work with no opportunity to familiarize themselves with information technology
- mostly middle managers

Trends like these should always be investigated and appropriate steps should be taken to reverse the situation.

The key points are that human resource planning involves:

- understanding the **internal factors,** which are those that arise from the priorities and realities of the organization itself:
    - short-term and long-term objectives and strategies
    - short-term operational requirements
    - production technologies
    - marketing plans
- understanding the **external factors**, which are:
    - national economical policy
    - likely changes in the international economy
    - likely changes in the labour market
- recognizing that, no matter which combination of techniques you use to identify the number and types of staff you are likely to need, there is no sure-fire method of accurately predicting your future staffing requirements

Once you know that you do, in fact, need to appoint additional staff – the next challenge is to ensure, as far as possible, that you appoint the right people.

What happens when you appoint the wrong person?

Recruiting and selecting the right person for the job can (and usually is) a long drawn-out procedure which takes a considerable amount of time, money, energy and hard work. At the end of the process, if you have been diligent, careful, cautious and exacting you **may** have chosen the right person. But, if you have been cavalier, slapdash, hasty (or unlucky) you will, probably, have chosen the **wrong** person. So, if you make an unwise choice it is something you will have live with and regret, possibly on a daily basis, for a long time to come.

ACTIVITY 2

List three negative effects which you, your team or your organization might experience as a direct result of selecting the wrong person for the job.

1   You

2   Your team

3   Your organization

FEEDBACK

The effects of recruiting the wrong person can be many and various, including:

Effects on you, as someone involved in the recruitment process
- personal loss of confidence ('I made a bad decision')
- public loss of confidence ('What was she/he thinking of?')

Effects on you, as team leader
- 'carrying' someone on the team
- possible extra personal workload to make up for the 'wrong' person's inefficiency
- additional stress caused by having to manage conflict situations within the team – due to the 'wrong' person's inability to do the job or fit into the team

Effects on the team

■ resentment, low morale and de-motivation (due to increased workload)

■ missed deadlines and objectives (due to lack of input or inappropriate input from the new recruit)

■ conflict (amongst team members, or directed towards you as team leader)

Effects on the organization

■ missed deadlines, budget allocations exceeded, poor quality control, lowering of quality standards, loss of competitive advantage, bad press, loss of reputation and credibility

Giving yourself every opportunity to recruit the right person

No system is infallible. Even if you follow all of the right procedures and exercise the utmost care and caution you may still, with the best of intentions, make a mistake. But, if you follow the advice given in this workbook, there is less chance of making a mistake. You will stack the odds in your favour rather more than if you approached recruitment and selection without due care and attention.

WHAT'S THE JOB?

You can recruit in many different ways:

■ advertising in a newspaper or journal

■ advertising 'in-house' to existing staff

■ employing a 'head-hunting' or specialist recruitment agency

■ networking amongst colleagues and word-of-mouth

No matter which process you use, you will be likely to attract a number of applicants, all of whom would 'like the job' and 'consider themselves right for the job'. The hardest part of the recruitment process is not getting people to apply, but in choosing the most suitable person from amongst all the applicants.

The first step you need to take is to get very clear about the job to which you hope to appoint someone. Many organizations use the expertise within their human resource or training departments to create a suitable Job Description for new vacancies. Sometimes this results in old, out-of-date Job Descriptions being fished out of the filing cabinet and used as the basis for selecting the right candidate.

ACTIVITY 3

Currently, within your organization, what methods are used for collecting and collating the information which, when put together, will result in an appropriate job description?

FEEDBACK

Most organizations use some mix of the following methods to gather information about the tasks, duties and responsibilities involved in individual jobs:

■ observation of the job holder at work by either (a) staff from the human resource function within the organization or (b) specialist job analysts brought in to work in a consultancy capacity
■ interviews with the job holder
■ diaries kept by the job holder
■ questionnaires completed by the job holders and those colleagues who most often interact with the job holder
■ critical incident recording by both the job holder and those colleagues who were also involved in the critical incident. A critical incident is one where (a) everything went absolutely right and the experience provides an example of behaviour which be repeated in the future, or (b) everything went disastrously wrong and the experience provides a template for actions and behaviours which should, at all costs, be avoided in the future.

No matter how the information is gathered, a valid and useful Job Description will clearly define the nature of the job and the kind of work which the job holder will be expected to do on a daily basis, as part of their normal duties. The document should provide details of:

■ The **main** responsibilities and activities involved
The specific responsibilities relating to:
a Personnel. This is about the lines of authority. For whom will the job holder be responsible?

b   Resources. This may mean money, equipment, space. What are the resources for which the job holder will be responsible? Is there a 'top-line' for the budget, or is it open-ended?

c   Planning. This may be short-term or long-term. Will the job holder be responsible for short-term planning at, say, team or departmental level? Or will they also be involved in long-term strategic planning?

d   Decisions. This is about the extent of the job holder's authority. What decisions will the job holder be empowered to make? When/where is the boundary between the job holder's power to make decisions, and their manager's power to make or veto decisions?

■   Supervision. To whom will the job holder report?

■   Contacts. To what extent will the job holder be required to network outside the company? To which external companies, organizations, agencies will the job holder be representing their employer?

■   Working conditions. Will the job holder be based in a static location, or will they be expected to travel? Is the job (and the working environment) fairly sedate, with flexible deadlines (perhaps requiring an analytical approach); or fast and frenetic (requiring a pro-active, high energy approach).

ACTIVITY 4

Complete the chart below with sufficient detailed information to provide an accurate Job Description of your own job.

A Main responsibilities and activities
B Specific responsibilities 1 Personnel. Responsible for: 2 Financial Resources. Responsible for: 3 Planning. Responsible for: 4 Decision Taking: Responsible for:
C Supervision
D Contacts
E Working conditions

WHAT KIND OF PERSON DO YOU NEED TO DO THE JOB?

A carefully prepared Job Description will describe the job in considerable detail. The advantages of having a document like this are that:

■ you (and everyone else involved in the recruitment process) knows what the requirements, demands, difficulties and rewards of the job are likely to be

---

A **Main responsibilities and activities**
- Evaluating previous and existing training programmes
- Undertaking Training Needs Analysis throughout the company
- Updating and delivering existing training courses to staff throughout the company
- Designing and delivering new training courses to staff throughout the company
- Implementing Investors in People and NVQs throughout the company
- Where appropriate, identifying appropriate external training suppliers
- Advising the board on new training initiatives and opportunities for management development

B **Specific responsibilities**
1 Personnel. Responsible for:
- the appointment and supervision of appropriate external training suppliers
- the work of one Training Co-ordinator
2 Financial Resources. Responsible for:
- management of the Training budget allocation (which will not exceed £175 000.00)
- negotiation and management of payments to external contractors and training suppliers
3 Planning. Responsible for:
- scheduling training delivery throughout the company (in the UK)
- planning appropriate training events which will enable:
    (a) training participants to work towards and gain NVQs
    (b) the company to work towards and gain IIP accreditation
- keeping abreast of new training initiatives and planning to meet their requirements
4 Decision Taking: Responsible for:
- Evaluating the results of Training Needs Analysis
- Evaluating usefulness of previous and existing training interventions
- Exercising judgement as to type and length of future training interventions

C **Supervision**
- Will work to the Human Resources & Training Director (with considerable personal flexibility of operation within the constraints imposed by the requirement to work as a team member)
- Can expect to see supervisor infrequently

D **Contacts**
- The post involves extensive liaison with the board, company staff at all levels, external consultancies and suppliers (including Colleges of Higher and Further Education), TECs, Chambers of Commerce, Institute of Management, Institute of Personnel & Development, other training and human resource professionals

E **Working conditions**
- Based in head office in Milton Keynes but involving extensive travel to, and work within, stores and offices throughout the country
- Demanding, fast-moving environment
- Highly paced work involving tight schedules and deadlines and reconciliation of competing demands from different sources

---

Figure 1 Job Description for a Training Officer

- prospective candidates can see at a glance whether or not they have the necessary skills, knowledge and experience

Even so, a Job Description by itself is not enough. You also need a Person Specification. This document should describe the personal skills, qualities, attributes and experience which the job holder should possess. The best Person Specifications have two columns:

- a column which describes the **essentials**
- a column which describes the **desirables**

In a perfect world, the person appointed to the job would have all the essential skills and qualities, plus all the desirable skills and qualities. In real life, if you can find someone with all the essentials plus one or two of the desirables, then it's likely that you've found someone who stands a reasonably good chance of doing the job to the required standard. An example of a Person Specification, prepared for the Training Officer job, described in Figure 1, is shown in Figure 2.

	Essential	Desirable
Physical qualities	■ Good health ■ Smart, professional appearance ■ Capable of working long hours under pressure	
Education	■ Degree	■ IPD or other appropriate training qualification ■ Membership Institute Personnel & Development ■ Membership Institute of Management
Training/Skills	■ In-depth knowledge and understanding of Investors in People and NVQs	■ NVQ Assessor Award
Intelligence	■ Ability to analyse and process large amounts of data	■ Able to create imaginative and innovative training solutions
Special aptitudes	■ Excellent communication skills – able to convey complex information to wide audience ■ Computer literate ■ Clean driving licence	■ Experience of presenting at Board level ■ Experience of Windows '95, Pagemaker and Word for Windows 6 ■ Working knowledge of French and German
Disposition	■ Able to influence and persuade ■ Good team player ■ Leadership skills ■ Drive and initiative ■ Proactive and willing to respond to a range of challenges	■ Extensive network of contacts within industry and training & development
Interests	■ Psychology	■ NLP
Personal circumstances	■ Free to travel away from home to meet the demands of the job ■ Willing to work flexible hours	

Figure 2 Person specification for the job of Training Officer

Complete the chart below to prepare a Person Specification either for your own job, or for a current vacancy which you are seeking to fill within your organization.

	Essential	Desirable
Physical qualities		
Education		
Training/skills		
Intelligence		
Special aptitudes		
Disposition		
Interests		
Personal circumstances		

Finding your perfect person

Describing your perfect person (through the process of Identifying the skills, knowledge and experience required) is your first step on the rocky road to actually filling the vacancy. Once you are sure you have described your ideal candidate on paper, the next step is advertise the job.

ADVERTISING IN-HOUSE

If you work in a large organization where, perhaps, there are many units located in different parts of the country (or the world) then it may certainly be worth advertising the vacancy in-house.

NETWORKING

You may already know someone (currently working elsewhere) who would be an ideal 'fit'. Even if your Perfect Person doesn't immediately spring to mind, there's no harm in asking around and advertising the vacancy by word-of-mouth.

CASE STUDY

Peter, CEO of an electrical engineering company, explains how this approach worked for him.

'I needed to find a replacement for my IT Director and I happened to mention this to a colleague when we met at a conference in Brussels.

He said he thought Jim, his IT manager currently working in Brussels, might be suitable. Jim's wife had been offered an outstanding career opportunity in the UK and so the family were preparing to relocate back home. I set up a meeting – Jim matched the Person Specification almost perfectly and he jumped at the chance. It was ideal for both of us – appointing Jim saved me a lot of time and money which I might have had to spend on recruitment, and Jim was delighted to have found a job which met all of his criteria with regard to location, salary and so on.'

RECRUITMENT AGENCIES AND EXECUTIVE SEARCH CONSULTANCIES (HEAD-HUNTERS)

The main drawback with recruitment and head-hunting consultancies is that unless you have prepared thoroughly, you may be swamped by hundreds of unsuitable applicants. The best way to side-step this situation is to come up with precise specifications regarding both the job (Job Description) and the kind of person you need for the job (Person Specification).

Give the agency or consultancy clear guidelines about:

- the maximum number of CVs you are prepared to consider
- the interviewing procedure, e.g. first interview, shortlist interview, final selection interview
- the time-scale, e.g. commence interviews first week in June, appoint by last week in July

and do make sure that you totally understand how much you will be expected to pay, in total, for their consultancy services.

NEWSPAPER AND/OR JOURNAL ADVERTISING

The medium you choose for your recruitment advertisements will depend on the type of vacancy. For example, if you're looking for a secretary you might choose your local evening newspaper; if you're looking for a training officer you might choose *People Management*, the IPD Journal; if you're looking for a Communications Director you might choose the *Guardian* or one of the Sunday papers. The key point to remember is that you need to spell out, in your advertisement:

- what the job entails
- the skills, qualifications and experience that are required

Describing exactly the kind of person you need in a clear and straightforward advertisement can save you a great deal of time. It is far better to have twenty applicants all of whom, in some way, match your requirements, rather than 500 unsuitable applicants.

Screening application forms and CVs

APPLICATION FORMS

Some organizations prefer job applicants to complete their own company-designed application form. This allows the organization to ask candidates to provide, on the form, specific information which might be omitted from a CV. For example:

- Are you fluent in any languages other than English?
- Do you hold any public office?
- Do you need a work permit?

Figure 3 is an example of a Job Application which asks the most usual, standard questions.

POSITION FOR WHICH YOU ARE APPLYING
Title (Ms, Mrs, Mr, Dr) Surname: First names:
Address: Post code:
Telephone:
Education:
Qualifications:
Languages other than English? To what level?
Membership of Professional Bodies or Associations:
Employment History (*please include dates, salary, job responsibilities and most important achievements*)
Current salary? Expected salary?
Current driving licence details: Details of all endorsements:
Do you hold any public office? (e.g. JP, councillor etc.)
Do you have any disabilities? (If so, please give details)
Are you registered disabled? (If so, please give Registered no.)
Hobbies and interests:
Additional information in support of your application:
Names and addresses of two referees:

Figure 3   Example of a standard Job Application

CURRICULUM VITAE

Many candidates prefer to prepare their own CV (over which they have total control) and send this with a covering letter. Much important information can be gleaned from the way in which the CV has been prepared, and the quality and quantity of information which has been disclosed.

Anyone who is **serious** about applying for a job will do their utmost to ensure that their CV is well presented and makes a good impression. Watch out for:

■ Torn or grubby CVs, or those which contain numerous spelling mistakes. Good spelling may not be necessary for the job, but you could reasonably expect a serious candidate to either personally check the spelling (using a dictionary) or enlist the aid of someone else to carry out this task on their behalf. Key question – If a torn or grubby CV is an example of their best shot, how are they likely to perform on the job on a cold Monday morning, six months after they've been appointed?

- Are there major gaps in the dates between employment? There may be a perfectly valid reason for this, such as time out to raise a family, for example. Or there may be other, less acceptable reasons. If there are gaps and the applicant otherwise seems like they could be your Perfect Person, simply note the dates and ask about the gaps at interview.

Checklist for screening application forms and CVs

Application forms
- Has the candidate answered **all** the questions?
- Is there sufficient, detailed information?
- Is the standard of presentation (cleanliness, legibility, spelling etc.) what you would expect from a candidate applying for this level/type of vacancy?
- Are there major, unexplained gaps in the education or employment history?

CVs
- Is there sufficient, detailed information?
- Is the standard of presentation (cleanliness, legibility, spelling etc.) what you would expect from a candidate applying for this level/type of vacancy?
- Are there major, unexplained gaps in the education or employment history?
- Has the candidate offered the names and addresses of referees? Do they appear current and relevant?

Sorting the wheat from the chaff

By the closing date (the date, specified by you, by which all applications must be received), you will probably have a pile of forms, letters and/or CVs to consider. At this stage you need to put on your Ruthless Hat and separate the applications into three separate piles:

- Pile 1 Looks like this might be the Perfect Person
- Pile 2 Doesn't seem like this is my Perfect Person, but you never know
- Pile 3 No! No! No!

Pile 1 (which will probably be the smallest) will consist of those applications which most closely match your Person Specification in terms of skills, knowledge, qualifications and experience. These people will have all (or nearly all) of the essential qualities plus, perhaps, one or two of the desirables.

Pile 2 will contain applications from candidates who almost match the Person Specification but who, maybe, do not have all the qualifications or experience you feel are necessary. Even so, if no one in pile 1 turns out to be suitable, you may be able to fill your vacancy with someone you have assigned to this pile.

Pile 3 (which may well be the largest pile) will consist of applications from people who do not appear to have read your advertisement, and who do not match your Job Description or Person Specification in any way at all.

One-to-one or panel interview?

You may decide to interview candidates:

- in a one-to-one situation, you and the applicant alone, face to face
- in a panel or board situation, you plus a group of colleagues, face to face with the applicant

Each approach has its own advantages and disadvantages, and these need to be taken into consideration before making a final decision about the interview format.

ACTIVITY 6

List two advantages, for the candidate, of a **one-to-one** interview.

1

2

List two advantages, for the candidate, of a **board** or **panel** interview.

1

2

FEEDBACK

The **advantages**, for the candidate, of a one-to-one interview:

- Usually less formidable and, therefore, less stressful than a panel or board
- Usually easier for the candidate to create rapport and establish some kind of positive relationship with just one person
- In the right circumstances, the candidate and the interviewer can establish a pace and style which suits them both

The **advantages**, for the interviewer, of a one-to-one interview:

- Talking to just one person, the candidate is more likely to relax, 'open up' and display their true personality
- The interviewer can steer the interview in the direction they choose and focus on areas which are, from their point of view, of particular interest or importance
- If the interviewer is to line-manage the candidate they can, hopefully, select someone who not only has the skills and experience to do the job, but is also someone with whom they can get along

The **advantages**, for the candidate, of a board or panel interview:

- Even if one person on the panel takes against them (for whatever reason) they still stand a good chance of impressing the remainder of the panel
- Different people are likely to be interested in different aspects of the candidate's background and abilities. Rather than focusing on just one area or topic, there is likely to be a broader range of enquiry. The candidate may have the opportunity to discuss a wide range of matters and so compensate for any apparently doubtful areas of expertise or experience.

The **advantages**, for the interviewers, of a board or panel interview:

- No one person has to take sole responsibility for appointing or not appointing a candidate
- Different people can bring different skills to the interview panel. Sometimes (depending on the level of the job) panels consist of people with a range of different interests. For example, a panel might consist of:
    - the MD or CEO of the company
    - the Human Resource or Training Manager
    - the person who will be the successful candidate's line-manager
    - a representative of the team which the successful candidate will be joining, e.g. someone from the accounts department who will work alongside the successful candidate
    - one or more people with specialist knowledge, e.g. a lawyer, an accountant, a chemist, an engineer, who can ask the tricky specialist questions
- The people on the panel who have the most interviewing experience can lead the way and set the scene for everyone
- Even if one person on the panel displays an irrational hostility towards a good candidate, the rest of the panel can make sure that common sense prevails

The main **disadvantages** of one-to-one interviews are:

- If the interviewer is inexperienced, a good candidate may slip through the net simply because of a failure to ask the right kinds of questions
- Sometimes people can get off to a bad start and, in a short one-to-one interview, it's often difficult to mend fences and put things right

The main **disadvantages** of panel or board interviews are:

- Individual panel members can get out of hand, take over and try to control the process. This is neither useful nor helpful for anyone and can be very intimidating for the candidate
- If everyone on the panel asks numerous questions which require detailed answers, the interviews can last forever
- Gathering a panel can often be difficult in terms of synchronizing diaries, and it is certainly expensive in terms of time (five people, earning an average of £15 per hour, interviewing for eight hours each day, for three days = £1800)
- The successful candidate's future line manager may be intimidated by more senior members of the panel; may feel that they have not had a genuine opportunity to ask questions of particular importance to them; and may even be saddled with someone they really don't want because of the group's decision.

CASE STUDY

Susan, a Director of Studies in a College of Further Education describes her experience of panel interviewing:

'We needed to appoint a Lecturer to teach Art & Design within my Directorate. The Principal set up the panel which consisted of himself, another Director of Studies, an IT Lecturer – don't ask me why – and myself. We didn't, as a panel, prepare for the interviews. There was no discussion about the process or the kinds of questions we would each ask. In the end the Principal, as the most senior person, just took over the proceedings … it was a nightmare … none of us felt that we'd had an opportunity to get to know any of the candidates or assess their abilities. We couldn't agree about anything and so, in the end, we didn't appoint anyone. It was a complete waste of time.'

ACTIVITY 7

What advice could you give that might have made this panel interview more productive?

The key points here are, if you are going to run panel or board interviews:

- gather the right mix of people to sit on the panel
- prior to the interviews discuss the process, and make sure that everyone is clear about:
  - the amount of time which is to be allocated to each candidate
  - the areas of interest for which each interviewer will be personally responsible – e.g. past history? future ambitions? specialist knowledge?
- make sure that everyone on the panel is given an equal opportunity to contribute to the process – otherwise they will feel as though they are there to simply make up the numbers and will quickly become bored and impatient

Setting the stage

Where you actually hold the interviews will depend on the level of the job to be filled, the number of applicants, the amount of time available for the interview process and whether you choose the one-to-one or panel interview format. For a fairly junior post you may decide that one-to-one interviews in your office are most appropriate; whilst for senior appointments you may feel that a panel interview held in the company's Board Room, or even in an hotel, are most appropriate.

ACTIVITY 8

Cast your mind back over your own career and identify the **worst** interview you have attended as a candidate, and the **best** interview. What made the difference between a good interview and a bad interview?

I   The **worst** interview I ever experienced as a candidate sticks in my mind because:

2   The **best** interview I ever experienced as a candidate was particularly good because:

FEEDBACK

Everyone who has attended interviews can relate their own horror stories, and also their own version of the magic interview they sailed through and got the job. Your own experiences can teach you a great deal about what to do and what to avoid as the person in the interviewing seat.

NO INTERRUPTIONS OR DISTRACTIONS

Whichever format and venue you choose, do make sure that you are not disturbed by anything or anyone during the interview process. Hold all telephone calls, close down your pager or mobile 'phone and alert your secretary or a colleague to the fact that you are **not available**. Interruptions and distractions will not only break your concentration but will also send a clear signal to the candidates that:

■ they are not very important
■ the job is not very important
■ you don't really care whether or not you get the right person for the job

PREPARE THOROUGHLY

Read and memorize both the Job Description and the Person Specification. Make sure that you have a copy of both documents with you during the interview so that, if necessary, you can refresh your memory.

ESTABLISH RAPPORT

Some people get tense at interviews. Some people lose all sense of proportion and get so nervous they can hardly remember their own name. Part of your task is to establish a good rapport with each candidate so that, hopefully, you will get the best out of the meeting.

Welcome each person pleasantly, introduce yourself and make sure that you get their name right. Pay attention to the seating arrangements and, if you can, try to organize seats which are all at the same level and preferably side by side. If you do have to sit opposite candidates, try to face people across a low coffee table or a meeting table. (If you really want to intimidate someone, make them feel ill at ease and spoil their chances of presenting themselves in the best light, give them a low seat which is difficult to get in and out of, and face them across a wide expanse of desk. That should do the trick nicely.)

Aim to be relaxed, interested, well-mannered and non-critical. Listen carefully and don't interrupt candidates when they are answering questions.

You will find out what you really need to know only if you ask the right questions. Make sure that you have a suitable list for each candidate.

ACTIVITY 9

List three aspects of the candidate's ability to do the job which you need to question:

1

2

3

FEEDBACK

You will need to find out about the candidate's:

- technical or specialist knowledge or expertise
- intelligence and ability to think clearly, analyse and reason and use their initiative
- communication skills
- motivation
- attitude to team working
- leadership or management skills (where this is appropriate for the vacancy)

STANDARD QUESTIONS

Make a list of the questions you plan to ask. Begin the interview with a range of standard questions. Most candidates worth their salt will have prepared standard answers so, although these lines of enquiry will allow you both to settle in to the process, they are unlikely to give you any real in-depth information.

Checklist of standard interview questions

- Tell me something about yourself and your career to date
- Which aspects of your current (or last) post did you find most enjoyable? (Or, most challenging?)
- Where do you see yourself in five years' time?
- What is it about joining this particular company which appeals to you most?
- What special qualities or skills will you bring to this job?
- What would you say are your two main strengths? (And/or your two main weaknesses?)
- Why should we appoint you?
- If you were appointed, what changes would you like to implement?
- What are your ambitions?
- How would you describe your main achievements in your career to date?

PROBING QUESTIONS

If you are satisfied with the answers you have been given in response to the standard questions, then it's time to move on to the probing questions. You will need to carefully prepare these in advance as the questions you ask will very much depend on the type and level of job for which you are interviewing. Probing questions can help you to find out about the real quality of the candidate.

Many people, at interview, simply fall apart with nerves. The shaking, stammering, drooling wreck sitting in front of you may, in fact, be a highly competent professional ... when not facing up to the ordeal of an interview situation. Conversely, the smooth, slick individual who answers your standard questions confidently and easily may not be able to deal with the cut-and-thrust of real life. The interview is your only opportunity to find out what each person is really like, how they think and how they are likely to perform on the job. Unexpected, probing questions, based on 'What if?' scenarios are a good way to obtain genuine, unrehearsed responses. Some examples, which you can adapt to suit your own organization and circumstances, are given in the next checklist.

Checklist examples of probing questions

- What if a major client threatened to withdraw their account because of the unprofessional behaviour displayed by a member of your team ... how would you handle the situation?
- What if there was a total breakdown of the network and we lost all our data – plus backups – what would you do?
- What if you discovered insider trading (or some other unethical business practice) on your team ... how would you deal with it?
- WHAT IF, through no fault of your own, you discovered your departmental spending had gone £100K over budget ... how would you rectify the situation?
- WHAT IF you found out that a member of your team was having problems with substance abuse at work ... what would you do?
- WHAT IF you found out that a major consignment was unfit to be shipped to an important client and the deadline was tomorrow – how would you handle it?

THE CANDIDATE'S QUESTIONS

Prepare in advance to answer questions from candidates:

- Does the company run an appraisal system, and how does it work?
- What are the lines of authority? To whom do I report and who reports to me?
- Does the company have any plans for expansion into Europe?
- Why did the previous post-holder leave?
- What kind of opportunities are there for training and development?

Beware candidates who only ask questions like:

- How soon can I take some holiday?
- I'm finishing an Open University course – will the company pay for it?
- I won't be expected to work overtime will I?

RECORD THE DETAILS

Schedule the appointment times so that you have at least ten minutes free time between each candidate. Use this time to record the details of each interview so that, at the end of the process, you can check back and compare one applicant against another. Figures 4 and 5 are two examples of forms which you could use to note down your impressions at the end of each interview.

CANDIDATE'S NAME: Ben Scott DATE OF INTERVIEW: 25 June 1996 VACANCY: Systems Controller				
	EXCELLENT	GOOD	FAIR	UNACCEPTABLE
APPEARANCE	✓			
COMMUNICATION SKILLS		✓		
TECHNICAL OR SPECIALIST KNOWLEDGE	✓			
DETERMINATION/ MOTIVATION		✓		
INTEGRITY/ PRINCIPLES/ETHICS		✓		
INNOVATIVE/ CREATIVE/IMAGINATIVE			✓	
ANALYTICAL/ LOGICAL THOUGHT		✓		
TEAM PLAYER		✓		
LEADERSHIP QUALITIES			✓	

Figure 4   Candidate assessment form, example 1

Sometimes selecting the right person for the job is easy. There's one candidate who stands head and shoulders above all the rest and you just **know** you have found your Perfect Person. Sometimes, making the right decision is much more difficult.

CANDIDATE'S NAME: *Marianne Temple*				
DATE OF INTERVIEW: *12 August, 1996*				
VACANCY: **Sales Clerk**				
CRITERIA	(a) Excellent	(b) Good	(c) Fair	(d) Poor
Your own criteria for the job, e.g ■ knowledge of Windows '95	✓			
■ previous retail experience	✓			
■ appearance		✓		
■ references	✓			
TOTALS:	3	1		

OVERALL ASSESSMENT:
a Outstanding – excellent candidate   3
b Suitable – good candidate   1
c Doubtful – unlikely candidate   0
d Unacceptable   0

Comments: *Excellent candidate*

Figure 5   Candidate assessment form, example 2

ACTIVITY 10

Consider the following situation:

Two candidates, Joanna and Paula, both have the knowledge, skills and experience to do the job, and both of them meet your Person Specification equally well.

How would you make your decision?

FEEDBACK

The key point here is if you are not sure, do nothing straight away! If you aren't absolutely certain that you have found the right person, don't make a decision until you have explored some other options. When indecision strikes you have four main choices:

- use your intuition
- set up another interview
- use some form of recognized testing
- run an assessment centre

Intuition

If you genuinely feel that you have seen two or more candidates who seem equally perfect for the job, then use your intuition or 'gut-feeling' to help you decide. Trust your instincts to tell you which candidate will fit best into the team; which candidate you will enjoy working with the most; which candidate will make the major contribution to your organization.

Set up another interview

If necessary:

- call the candidates back for a second (or even third) interview (you might consider asking a trusted colleague to sit in with you to give their opinion of the candidates)
- organize a panel or board interview

Don't feel embarrassed that you can't reach an immediate decision. Colleagues will be flattered if you consult and involve them; they will feel let down if you appoint the wrong person. Mistakes can be costly, frustrating and even damaging for you, your team, your organization. Once someone is appointed you may be stuck with them for a very, very long time.

In a situation where you don't have even one suitable candidate, re-advertise and go through the process all over again. In the long run, it will be worth the extra effort.

Testing

Psychometric and psychological testing (the terms are inter-changeable and both mean the same thing) is a very specialized area. Most of the tests, which can only be run by 'licensed users' have to be returned to the point of origin for scoring. Many organizations use testing as a regular part of their recruitment and selection process. If this is not the case in your company, you might think it appropriate to advocate the introduction of testing (maybe if lots of 'poor' recruitment decisions have been made), or if you face a one-off situation where you just can't choose between two or more people.

Psychometric and psychological testing tests the candidate's ability to solve problems, perform tasks or make judgements. These tests look at intelligence, ability, aptitude, language development, perception, personality, temperament and disposition, interests, habits, values and preferences.[1]

Details of consultants with specialist knowledge of psychometric testing can be obtained from:

- Institute of Management (Research Department), tel.: 01536 204222
- British Psychological Society, tel.: 0116 254 9568

Assessment centres

Assessment centres, which are often time consuming and expensive to set up and run, are used to evaluate candidates for key posts, usually where there are a significant number of applicants for a job. It would be quite unusual to set up an assessment centre for just one or two people.

Assessment centres are usually organized by external, specialist consultants, and may be run in-house on your own premises, or at an external, specialist venue. Job candidates are required to undertake numerous activities, each of which is observed and continuously evaluated. Depending on the job and the organization's requirements, the activities might be held indoors, outdoors or some combination of the two.

Indoor activities could include:

- group discussions or role-playing
- presentations
- 'in-tray', fact-finding and problem-solving exercises

Outdoor challenges could include:

- bridge building
- orienteering
- rescue and survival techniques
- and other fun-filled activities.

The whole point of assessment centres is to give the specialist consultants and senior company staff the opportunity to observe candidates over a period of time (anything from two to five days) performing under pressure, and often in difficult circumstances. A well-designed assessment centre will give observers a good opportunity to evaluate candidates' leadership, team-building and team-working skills.

Use the next activity as an opportunity to create a checklist which you can use as an *aide-mémoire* during and after the recruitment and selection process.

ACTIVITY 11   C8.2

Consolidate your learning by setting out – in order – the important processes and landmarks involved in recruitment:

FEEDBACK

You may have included some or all of the action points listed below:

■ Prepare detailed job analysis

■ Prepare detailed person specification

■ Choose recruitment method – in-house? newspaper? agency?

■ Decide on closing date

■ Select venue for interviews

■ Choose interview method – one-to-one or panel?

■ If panel interviews are to take place, select and brief panel members

■ Choose interview process – one interview? preliminary plus shortlist?

■ Prepare your own list of standard and probing questions

■ Prepare candidate assessment forms

■ Process applications

■ Invite selected candidates

■ Clear your diary for the appropriate amount of time

■ Conduct interviews

■ Select successful candidate

■ Inform all candidates of the result of the selection process

■ Prepare contract of employment

■ Arrange induction for the new member of staff

SUMMARY

- The four main approaches to medium and long-term human resource planning are:
  - managerial judgement
  - statistical analysis
  - work study
  - productivity measurement
- When planning ahead, account must always be taken of:
  - your organization's internal factors:
    - objectives and strategies
    - operational requirements
    - production technologies
    - marketing plans
  - the external factors:
    - national economic policy
    - changes in international economy
    - changes in the labour market
- The most usual sources of information which will enable you to prepare a reasonably accurate job description are:
  - observation of the current job holder
  - interviews with the job holder
  - diaries, questionnaires and critical incident reports completed by the job holder
- A comprehensive job description will include the following details:
  - activities and responsibilities – what will the job holder do?
  - lines of authority – for whom will the job holder be responsible?
  - resources for which the job holder will be responsible
  - extent of the job holder's planning and decision-making responsibilities
  - to whom will the job holder report?
  - to what extent will the job holder be expected to represent the organization to external companies and agencies?
  - what will working conditions be like?
- A person specification should describe the **essential** qualities, skills, knowledge and experience which the job holder must possess, plus the **desirable** qualities, skills, knowledge and experience which the employer would really like the job holder to possess.
- When screening application forms and CVs look carefully at:
  - presentation
  - amount of information
  - any unexplained gaps in education or employment history
  - whether or not the referees appear to be current and relevant

- If you decide to interview by panel make sure that:
  - each person on the panel is appropriate and will have something to contribute to the interview process
  - the panel is thoroughly briefed beforehand, so that each person is clear about the role they will take
  - **Standard** questions will allow the candidate to settle in to the interview and provide details of experience, background and so on – career to date? specialist knowledge? reasons for applying?
  - **Probing** questions will allow the candidate to discuss how they might respond in stressful, demanding, real-life situations.
- Make sure you take five or ten minutes at the end of each interview to record your impressions. If you don't do this straight away you can easily get confused about people, and may let a good candidate slip through your fingers.
- If you feel unsure, don't appoint. It is more sensible to re-advertise and go through the whole process again, than to appoint the wrong person and live to regret your mistake on a daily basis.

Notes

1 *British Psychological Society Bulletin* (1983) in Institute of Management, *Managing People*, Competent Manager Series (1995), p. 25.

Section 2 Discipline, grievance and redundancy procedures

Introduction

Investigating disciplinary matters, listening to employee grievances and explaining to staff that, for whatever reason, they are being made redundant, are all managerial responsibilities. You can't always anticipate when they are likely to occur, but you can prepare for them so that you know what to do if and when these situations arise.

In this section of the workbook we will be looking at how you can best tackle these situations by carrying out your responsibilities fairly and objectively whilst, at the same time, recognizing the pressure and stress these situations cause for the staff involved.

Discipline

If you have carefully worked your way through the recruitment and selection procedures outlined in Section 1, and if you have been both wise and lucky, you'll have selected the right person for the job. Hopefully, you will enjoy a long, peaceful and productive relationship. On the other hand, though, things may not work out as well as you had hoped.

Many situations will benefit from a counselling approach (discussed in Section 3). Hopefully, by using a range of interpersonal skills, a measure of understanding and some patience, you should be able to iron out most problems and get things back on track. Unfortunately, not all situations can be dealt with in this way. As a manager you will almost certainly, at some point in your career, be required to become involved in disciplinary proceedings against someone who works for your organization. Whatever the situation, you must always ensure that the action you take is:

- in-line with your organization's code of disciplinary practice and procedures
- in accordance with legal requirements. The relevant legislation which provides protection for employees is the Trade Union Reform and Employment Rights Act 1993 – often referred to as TURERA (which amends Employment Protection (Consolidation) Act 1978)

Code of disciplinary practice and procedures

Employers are required to give employees clear information about the disciplinary rules which apply to employees. This information allows everyone – employer, employee, union – to know the rules, systems and procedures which will be applied if and when disciplinary action is thought to be necessary.

The key point here is to make sure that, before you do anything, you thoroughly understand your company's code of disciplinary procedures, and that you are absolutely clear about the legal requirements. Failure to follow these two simple rules can cost your organization a considerable amount of money, and can cause you a great deal of embarrassment and numerous sleepless nights. If you do it wrong employees have the legal right to take their case for unfair dismissal to an Industrial Tribunal. If the Tribunal agrees with the employee that they have, in fact, been unfairly dismissed, then the Tribunal can require the employer to make one or more of the following payments to the employee:

- a basic award which covers the period from the date of dismissal to the hearing – £210 per week for up to a maximum of 30 weeks: maximum award £6300
- a compensatory award to reflect the employee's loss – maximum £11 300
- an additional award for failure to comply with a reinstatement or re-engagement order – maximum £5460
- total maximum which could be awarded by the Tribunal: £23 060

In addition, if the employer fails to reinstate or re-engage the employee following an unfair dismissal on the grounds of trade union membership, the employee could be awarded an additional two years' salary.

INDUSTRIAL TRIBUNALS

Industrial tribunals will hear cases brought by employees (who have two years' service) against their employers in respect of:

- unfair dismissal
- problems with contracts of employment
- health and safety

Employees do not need to have two years' service if they wish to be heard on matters relating to racial or sex discrimination.

Taking disciplinary action

CASE STUDY

Steve, the manager of an Executive Recruitment Agency, explains how his failure to follow the rules almost cost him his job:

'I received complaints from a couple of clients about a member of staff. I had experienced difficulties with this person previously and I had spoken to her, at great length, about the problems on more than one occasion, and I had given her a final warning. When two of my most important, influential and lucrative accounts complained, I felt that enough was enough. I dismissed her. Unfortunately I hadn't kept any record of our previous conversations, all of which had taken place privately, with just the two of us in my office. The final interview at which I dismissed her took place in the evening, when just the two of us were on the premises. It was the end of a very busy day and I took the only opportunity available to me … big mistake. Next thing a solicitor's letter arrived which explained that the employee was complaining of unfair dismissal. Head Office didn't want the bad press, I didn't have any paperwork or witnesses to substantiate my side of the story and she received a cheque from the company which, for her, settled the matter. Unfortunately, I had to live with the consequences. It was made very clear to me that I was a whisker away from disciplinary proceedings myself.'

The next activity will give you an opportunity to think about some of the reasons why you might find it necessary to begin disciplinary proceedings against a member of staff.

ACTIVITY 12

List four reasons why an organization might feel it would be appropriate to commence disciplinary proceedings against an employee.

1

2

3

4

FEEDBACK

No matter how you might personally feel about it, you simply cannot take disciplinary action against someone because they are boring, boastful, anti-social, bad-tempered, obstinate or otherwise difficult to get along with.

Generally, it is possible to take disciplinary action against an employee only where you can prove genuine incompetence and inability to do the job. It's important to recognize that poor job performance can be held to be the responsibility of the employer due to:

- appointing a person who is unsuitable for the job
- failing to provide correct guidance or appropriate training
- choosing an inappropriate person for promotion
- substance abuse
- dishonesty
- disruptive or aggressive behaviour towards staff or customers
- harassment of staff or customers

Under the Trade Union Reform and Employment Rights Act 1993 (which amends Employment Protection (Consolidation) Act 1978) staff may be dismissed for one or more of the following five reasons:

1 Lack of ability, skill or qualifications
2 Misconduct
3 Dishonesty
4 Genuine redundancy
5 Other statutory enactments applying to the job, e.g. if the job holder lost his or her driving licence, needed to drive and could not continue to do the job without breaking the law

Most companies operate a formal disciplinary procedure which consists of three separate stages:

1 **Informal oral** warnings
2 **Formal oral** warning or, in serious cases, formal oral warnings which are **confirmed in writing.** (Formal warnings, oral and written, should clearly explain the nature of the offence and the likely consequences of further offences)
3 **Final written warning**, which should clearly explain the consequences if there is a recurrence; consequences may be suspension, dismissal or some other penalty

In all cases, whether you are issuing a formal or informal, oral or written warning, the member of staff is entitled to

- know the accusations which are being made against them. They should be given a clear explanation of the rules they have broken and how they have broken them; or they should be told which standards they are not meeting and the improvements they need to make in order to meet those standards
- be given an opportunity to explain themselves, refute the accusations and state their case
- be accompanied to any meetings by a colleague or trade union shop steward

Disciplinary interviews

Disciplinary interviews are extremely stressful for everyone concerned. The next activity will give you an opportunity to consider how staff might react to the prospect and the reality of a formal or informal disciplinary interview.

ACTIVITY 13

Listed below are a number of ways in which an employee might respond during the course of a disciplinary interview. Consider each possibility and tick all of the boxes which you think might apply:

During the course of a disciplinary interview, employees may respond by feeling:

	Yes, very likely	No, not very likely
Attacked	❑	❑
Angry	❑	❑
Anxious	❑	❑
Defensive	❑	❑

	Yes, very likely	No, not very likely
Enraged	❑	❑
Embarrassed	❑	❑
Frightened	❑	❑
Humiliated	❑	❑
Hurt	❑	❑
Hysterical	❑	❑
Intimidated	❑	❑
Irritated	❑	❑
Suspicious	❑	❑
Tearful	❑	❑
Threatened	❑	❑
Worried	❑	❑

FEEDBACK

Regardless of the person or the circumstances, during a disciplinary interview you can reasonably expect a member of staff to feel and display any or even **all** of these emotions.

Your challenge, as the interviewer, is to remain calm, even-tempered, objective and impartial. Your task is to present the facts and listen to the employee's response. Your key objectives should be to get to the truth and stick to the procedures.

SORT OUT THE FACTS

Before the interview takes place, make sure that you have the facts of the matter. Ask yourself:

- is this a genuine problem?
- does the person making the accusation of wrong-doing have some kind of hidden agenda?
- are there witnesses? If so, talk to them and take statements?
- is there documentary evidence? If so, take the originals into your possession, and also make photocopies

Once you are absolutely certain that there has been a breach of discipline you need to inform the employee:

- they are required to attend a disciplinary interview
- the kind of interview it is to be – formal or informal

- they are invited to bring a colleague or trade union representative with them, if they choose to do so
- the time, date and place of the interview

You should also, if possible, arrange to have a trusted and impartial colleague at the interview who can act as an objective observer. You will need to record what is said and agreed during the interview so your objective observer could be tasked with note-taking. You might prefer to ask your secretary to take notes, but on the strict understanding that everything said and done during the interview is totally **confidential.**

PRIOR TO THE INTERVIEW

Read through:

- all the notes you have made during your investigation
- reports and any other documentation
- the employee's file or personnel records

ARRANGING THE INTERVIEW

Agree time and place with the employee. The disciplinary interview should be held in a quiet, private place, behind closed doors, where there will not be any interruptions. Make sure there are sufficient chairs for everyone. If possible, arrange chairs of the same height around a table. Remember, the employee must have an opportunity to state their case. Intimidation will not help you to get to the truth.

DURING THE INTERVIEW

Start on time – don't keep people waiting around.

Greet the employee (and their representatives) pleasantly, and introduce everyone in the room by name. Also state why each person is there … 'Sandy Cole, who will be taking notes of what we say and agree; Harry Milne, Training Manager, who is here as an objective observer.'

Begin by stating what kind of interview is taking place:

- informal oral warning
- formal oral warning to be followed up in writing
- formal interview to investigate gross misconduct

Explain, in detail, **why** the interview is taking place – unacceptable behaviour, inability to do the job to the required standard, or whatever. Go through any documentary or other evidence that supports the accusation. Invite the employee to state their case, and listen with your full attention. If, having examined all the evidence and listened to the employee's side of the story, you are still convinced that disciplinary action is appropriate, then you should:

1   Explain to the employee the consequences of what they have done – 'because, for the second time in a month, you failed to change the canisters, the line was down for forty-eight hours. This cost the company over £75 000 and cost each member of staff on the line anything from £10 to £38 in lost overtime.'

2   Explain the action you are taking – 'I am giving you a formal verbal warning that this is unacceptable behaviour. This warning will be confirmed in writing and the details will be recorded in your personnel file. The details will remain on your file for 12 months. If, after that time, there are no further problems, then the details will be removed and that will be the end of the matter.'

3   Inform the employee of their right to appeal against the decision – 'You do, of course, have the right to appeal against this decision.' (The appeals procedure for your organization should be specified in the contract of employment.)

4   Explain the next step if the behaviour is repeated – 'As you know Tom, the next step is a final written warning.'

5   Explain, simply and clearly, what must happen in the future – 'I expect you to carry out all the duties in your job description, and that includes checking the canisters twice every day, and changing them when they are empty.'

6   Try to end the interview on a positive and encouraging note – 'I value your contribution to the company, and I really hope that this matter is going to end here. I have confidence in your future performance – and I think the important thing is to put this behind us and move on.' If you feel it is appropriate, offer whatever training or additional support you think could be helpful.

DISMISSAL INTERVIEW

Sometimes, despite warnings, unacceptable behaviour continues, and dismissal becomes necessary. Where you have reached the end-of-the-line with someone, for example:

■   their behaviour or attitude is totally unacceptable and despite repeated warnings there has not been any improvement, or

■   they are guilty of gross misconduct such as fraud, theft or physical violence

then you should act swiftly and unemotionally.

Make sure that you follow all of the procedures outlined above but, in addition:

- arrange for someone to be on hand to offer advice and support to the person who is going to be dismissed (ideally, this should be someone with counselling training and experience)
- prepare a brief script of what you are going to say; if things get out of hand, you can refer to this
- prepare a written summary of the terms you are offering: e.g. two weeks pay in lieu of notice, five days holiday pay, because the employee is unlikely to remember what was said
- explain the decision, but do not justify or apologize
- set a time limit for the interview – ten or fifteen minutes – and stick to it
- if the employee is distressed (and this is often the case) pass them on to the counsellor who should be waiting to offer guidance and support

AFTER THE INTERVIEW

Make sure that the notes taken during the interview are typed up as soon as possible. Although there is no legal requirement, you may want to ask the employee to sign the notes to confirm that they represent a true and fair description of the interview.

Make sure that the notes are placed into the employee's file and that they are dated, and that the outcome of the interview is clearly shown, e.g. oral warning 2 April 1995, formal oral warning with written confirmation 19 September 1995, final warning 4 January 1996, dismissal 12 March 1996.

Although it is important to look on the bright side, do remember that if there is further conflict or legal implications for the future, these interview notes may play a crucial part. It is important that they are accurate, and truthfully reflect everything that was said and agreed.

Disciplinary procedures checklist

- For breaches of discipline such as poor work performance, excessive absenteeism, persistent lateness etc., the usual procedure is investigation followed by either appropriate counselling or:
  - verbal warning
  - verbal warning confirmed in writing
  - final written warning
- For gross misconduct such as fraud, theft, violence etc., the usual procedure is investigation and suspension of the employee in question, followed by:
  - letter to the employee giving details of the offence and the evidence against them; date, time and place of the disciplinary hearing; plus notification that they are entitled to be accompanied by a colleague, union representative or legal adviser (for very serious matters), to present their own evidence and arguments

---

- hearing at which all the evidence and arguments are heard and carefully considered
- a decision. The employee may be dismissed without notice, and the decision may be given both verbally and in writing. The employee should be informed of their right to appeal

ACTIVITY 14   C15.2, C16.2

Create a checklist of things to do and things to remember which will act as an *aide-mémoire* when you have to take a member of your staff through the organization's disciplinary proceedings.

1   Note down your company's disciplinary procedures relating to oral, oral and written and final written warnings:

2   Note down the steps you would take when investigating a complaint made against a member of staff:

3   Note down:
   a   where you would hold disciplinary interviews:

   b   who you would ask to attend as an objective observer:

   c   who you would ask to take notes during the interview:

4   Note down the system and procedure you would use to make sure that the notes of the interview were swiftly typed up, agreed by the employee and held safely in their file:

Grievance procedures

Employee grievances can be about a wide range of different matters including:

- an individual's pay and/or working conditions – 'I'm not being paid the same rate as Frank, but we're doing the same job.'
- a group's pay and/or working conditions – 'All of us in the accounts department feel that we're getting a bad deal with regard to the new premises.'
- personal relationships – 'My manager doesn't like me and she's making it difficult for me to do my job.'

As a manager, you may have to handle grievances which cover a wide range of matters, and which involve either one person, or a group of people.

Most organizations have a simple procedure for dealing with staff grievances and this should be clearly explained in the contract of employment and/or the staff handbook. The procedure for dealing with grievances is usually:

- employee explains the grievance to their line manager, either verbally or in writing
- if the line manager is unable to settle the matter, the grievance is referred to a higher authority.
- if the higher authority (usually a senior manager) is unable to settle the matter, then it is referred to the final authority – who may be the MD, CEO or the board of directors

No matter where you are in this chain – line manager, higher authority, final authority – do make sure that you honour the employee's right to be heard. Grievances (which can often be fairly minor, but very important from the point of view of the employee making the complaint) are often brought to management's attention because of:

- breakdown of internal communication between individuals, departments or functions
- genuine misunderstandings
- interpersonal difficulties like rivalry, jealously or plain dislike

Your role as an arbitrator is to:

- listen carefully, attentively and non-judgementally. Often, all someone needs is a sympathetic ear so they can get their grievance off their chest
- ask as many questions as you need to make sure you thoroughly understand the situation

- summarize what has been said, to make sure that both you and the employee have the same understanding (listening, questioning and summarizing are covered in detail in Workbook 16 *Communication*)

Once you understand the grievance, the next step is to do something about it. Your options are:

- investigate further and then meet again with the employee and impart your decision
- make a decision there and then

The employee's options are:

- accept your decision and close the matter
- appeal to a higher authority

No matter what the nature of the grievance, your challenge is to follow the procedures, treat each employee with full attention, absolute honesty, fairness and impartiality and, finally, reach an objective decision. If you have done this and the employee decides to take the grievance to the next level, then don't feel that you have failed. Simply allow the employee to appeal against your decision (they have the right) and if you are over-ruled accept the decision gracefully. If your decision is upheld, do not treat this as a victory.

The outcome of a staff grievance should not be viewed as a victory or a defeat, no matter who 'wins'. Once the matter is settled, and a final decision is reached, you'll find that it will be to everyone's benefit to get things back to normal as quickly as possible. In some instances you may feel that you have to bite the bullet and say nothing, if a higher authority disagreed with your decision. Or, if the appeal failed, you may have to build some bridges in order to re-establish a good working relationship with the member of staff who brought the grievance in the first place. Either way, don't allow disagreements to simmer under the surface, as this will not be productive for anyone.

Redundancy – the most difficult task of all

Perhaps the most difficult thing you will ever be required to do, as a manager, is to face a colleague across a desk and inform them that they are going to be made redundant. Redundancy (often also called downsizing) is a bitter pill for anyone to swallow, but is particularly hard for people who have, over many years, worked loyally and efficiently.

When faced with the task of relaying such unwelcome information, as a manager, your role is two-fold:

1 Presenting the information clearly and accurately, and in accordance with both your organization's requirements, and the legal requirements in force at the time, and

2 Presenting the information with sensitivity towards, and with awareness of, the recipient's psychological and emotional needs

Of course, some people – after the initial shock has subsided – may respond positively to the prospect of being made redundant. This particularly applies where the person:

- has been thinking about moving on anyway
- can look forward to collecting a handsome cheque and is getting close to retirement age
- has adjusted to the idea by making a firm commitment to either changing track and starting a totally different career; or setting up their own business; or moving out of the UK; or returning to full-time training and education

Sadly, many people (particularly those in their late forties or fifties), perceive redundancy as the end of their working life.

CASE STUDY

Nigel, Personnel Director with a manufacturing company, describes his first experience of relaying news about forthcoming redundancies to his staff.

'I was under orders from the MD, to see people in my office and tell them what was going to happen. It didn't matter to them that we needed to downsize to become more competitive. All they knew and cared about was that, after fifteen or twenty years, they were going to lose their jobs. Many of the people I talked to were a lot older than I am. They thought, and probably rightly so, that it was going to be very hard to find alternative employment. It was a difficult time for everyone ... and I honestly can say it was as hard for me to tell them the bad news as it was for them to hear it. The only saving grace was that I was able to arrange for specialist career counselling for everyone who was going. At least that helped people to put a decent CV together, and take a realistic look at the labour market.'

The next activity will give you an opportunity to consider the steps any organization needs to take when it looks as though downsizing may have to be undertaken in the company.

ACTIVITY 15

For the purpose of this activity, imagine that your MD has put it to you that, in order to improve productivity, the company has to downsize. In effect, this means that 10 per cent of the existing work force will have to be made redundant. She has asked you to prepare a downsizing plan.

List two key points you would have to bear in mind as you begin to create the plan.

1

2

FEEDBACK

When faced with the prospect of implementing a redundancy (downsizing) programme the key points to bear in mind are:

- staff should be treated fairly and with sensitivity
- the programme should be implemented swiftly and efficiently

A MAJOR LIFE CHANGE

Redundancy represents, to most people, a major life change. Elizabeth Kubler-Ross has identified seven stages that someone experiencing a major change (such as redundancy) often has to work through. These stages are shown in Figure 6.

- Stage 1: Shock – People respond to a life-changing event like redundancy with shock, numbness and disbelief – 'I don't believe it … this can't be happening'
- Stage 2: Denial – People move into denying that the change is really going to take place – 'It won't really happen … It'll all blow over and we'll get back to normal'
- Stage 3: Frustration – People begin to realize that it **is** going to happen, and at this stage they get angry, aggressive and frustrated – 'I don't deserve this … why me? It's not fair … it should be someone else'

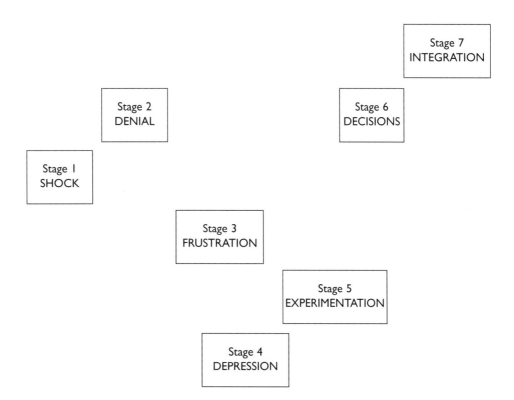

Figure 6 The stages most people experience during times of major life change

- Stage 4: Depression – People hit rock-bottom and can't really see the point of even trying to improve the situation – 'There's no point ... my life's over ... I'll never get another job'
- Stage 5: Experimentation – People can't bear the depression any longer and begin to wonder if, perhaps, there might be a way out of their dreadful situation – 'Anything's got to be better than feeling like this ... maybe I could look at some possibilities ... I suppose I have always fancied working for myself, maybe I should look into it a bit more'
- Stage 6: Decisions – People begin to make some decisions about their life (maybe just small ones to start with) and begin to feel a bit more optimistic and enthusiastic, although still cautious – 'No, working for myself isn't for me, but I am going to try for that job in Sheffield ... I might stand a chance'
- Stage 7: Integration – People begin to accept and integrate the change into their life – 'Well, we're going to go and see the children in Australia for a few weeks and then, when I get back, I'm going to start a carpet cleaning franchise. It's quite exciting really ... I'm looking forward to doing something different'

It is important to understand each of these stages, and how people are likely to respond:

- During your initial interview with someone, when you relay the bad news, don't be surprised if they respond quietly and have little to say, and few questions to ask. **Don't** think 'That went well! Perhaps they were expecting it.'

- When, later on, the same person seems to be acting perfectly normally without an apparent care in the world, **don't** make the mistake of thinking 'They're fine … they mustn't mind too much.'
- When the same person gets angry and aggressive, **don't** start to wonder 'What's happened to make them change?'
- When the same person changes yet again and becomes obviously withdrawn or depressed, **don't** assume that this is a permanent state of affairs, and **don't** feel guilty.
- During stage 5, even when new plans are made, expect them to be constantly revised and changed. Do your best to offer encouragement and support throughout the process. **Don't** lose patience and think 'the way he's chopping and changing his mind is driving me crazy … if he goes on like this he's never going to get anything sorted.'
- During stages 6 and 7, when the employee starts to make decisions, adjust to the change, and begin to look forward to the future; **don't** think 'Well, she's perfectly OK … always has been … all the worrying I did was a complete waste of time.

THE REDUNDANCY PLAN

The redundancy plan (usually a paper document), which sets out the way in which the downsizing is to be managed, should include details of:

- the number of staff who are to be made redundant – fifty people
- the location at which the staff are to be made redundant – twelve people at the Hartlepool site; twenty people at Bootle; eighteen people at Chester
- the dates when the redundancy programme is to start; and the date by which the programme is to be completed – commence 22 July 1996; completion by 22 December 1996
- details of how staff, trade unions and staff associations are to be informed about the programme – individual letter, signed by the MD to be sent to each member of staff; meetings to be arranged with Union representatives
- details of the financial arrangements for staff who volunteer to leave under the scheme – statutory payment plus 15 per cent
- details of the financial arrangements for key staff who volunteer, but whom the company does not wish to lose – loyalty payment of £5000 to retain key staff
- details of the financial arrangements for staff who face compulsory redundancy – statutory payment plus 5.5 per cent
- details of how selected staff members are to be informed about the way in which they are going to be individually affected; and how trade unions and staff associations are to be informed – initial group meeting with the MD and HR director; follow-up meetings with the Personnel Manager on an individual basis

The keys to success for everyone concerned – staff, unions and employers – are:

■ making sure that people have sufficient warning of what is going to happen. This will help staff not only to adjust to the future, but also give them time to look around for alternative employment

■ being open and honest with information, and keeping people informed on a regular basis. If there is not a good flow of information between staff and management, rumour and gossip will take off. Staff confidence and morale will be badly affected, with a knock-on effect on productivity and efficiency. Operating poor communication systems is not only unkind but also bad business practice. Generally, people are able to cope with truthful information (even if it is unpleasant) far better than they are able to cope with a constant stream of misinformation, rumour, innuendo and gossip

The next activity will give you an opportunity to consider the way in which you might begin to create a redundancy plan if this was to become necessary within your organization.

ACTIVITY 16

1 What measures could you take to avoid redundancies?

2 What criteria would you use for selecting staff who are to be made redundant?

FEEDBACK

Measures that can be taken to avoid redundancies include:

■ allowing for natural wastage. These are the people who are, for one reason or another, going to leave the company anyway. People who resign or retire are simply not replaced

■ eliminating overtime (or, if this is not possible, reducing overtime hours worked)

- dismissing subcontracted labour and taking on the work in-house
- developing a job-share programme which allows two people to share one job. This can be done by arranging for two people to work either alternate days or alternate weeks, or by splitting the day so that one person works in the morning, the other person works in the afternoon
- dismissing part-time staff
- organizing temporary lay-offs for full-time staff[1]

The most usual criteria used for selecting those staff who are to be made redundant is last in – first out. Although this criteria is the one usually favoured by the Unions (and staff) it doesn't always work well for the organization.

For example, say a company must lose one member of their office staff. The last person to join the company is the office supervisor; someone with extensive experience of information technology and systems and procedures. This person is considered to be a key member of staff. The person who has been a member of the office staff for the longest period of time is an accounts clerk with no IT or systems and procedures experience. Using the last in – first out criteria, the company would be expected to retain the services of the accounts clerk, and lose the office supervisor.

The company has to reserve the right to use another method of selection where choosing people for redundancy on the basis of service would affect the operational efficiency of the organization.

Dismissal for redundancy is deemed to be fair if:

- the redundancy is genuine and is not being used by the employer as an excuse for dismissing an incompetent member of staff
- the people who have selected for redundancy have been chosen using agreed criteria. The criteria may either be agreed within the company, or agreed with the trade union
- there is no suitable alternative work available. Rather than declare staff redundant, the organization is required to look for alternative work for these people, within the company
- redundancy selection does not contravene the Sex Discrimination or Race Discrimination Acts[2]

Career counselling

Career counselling (or outplacement consultancy) is a service which many firms purchase for the benefit of outgoing staff. Specialist consultants, often working in-house/on-site:

- interview outgoing staff members on a one-to-one basis

- provide assistance with job search and interview techniques
- help with the preparation of updated CVs

and, where necessary, provide counselling and emotional support. The costs and the range of services provided varies from consultancy to consultancy. A list of specialist consultancies who offer these services can be obtained from: Institute of Management Foundation, Management Information Centre, Management House, Cottingham Road, Corby, Northants NN17 1TT: Tel.: 01536 204222; Fax: 01536 201651.

Summary

- Disciplinary procedures must be carried out in accordance with your organization's Disciplinary Procedures as described in the Contract of Employment or Staff Handbook, **and** conform to the legal requirements described in the Trade Union Reform and Employment Rights Act 1993 (TURERA).
- Employees who have two years' service can take their case to an Industrial Tribunal if they feel they have just cause in relation to:
  - unfair dismissal
  - problems with their contract of employment
  - problems with health and safety
- Employees do not need to have two years' service if they are taking their case to an Industrial Tribunal on the grounds of:
  - sex discrimination
  - racial discrimination
- Under TURERA staff may only be dismissed for one or more of the following:
  - lack of ability, skill or qualifications
  - misconduct
  - dishonesty
  - genuine redundancy
  - other statutory enactments applying to the job, e.g. driver must be in possession of a driving licence
- Most organizations' disciplinary procedure consists of three stages:
  - oral warning
  - oral warning confirmed in writing
  - final written warning
- In all cases, employees must:
  - be told precisely what the accusations are which are being made against them
  - have the opportunity to put their own case forward

- be accompanied to any disciplinary meetings by a work colleague, trade union or staff association representative
- **Before** a disciplinary interview:
  - sort out the facts, take statements, obtain witness statements or written evidence where appropriate
  - inform the employee of the time, date and place of interview; the type of interview (informal or formal) and remind them they are entitled to be accompanied by a colleague/representative
  - arrange for an impartial observer to be present at the interview
  - gather together any notes you have made and be sure to read through the employee's personnel file
  - arrange for the interview to take place in a private setting where there will no distractions or disturbances
- **During** the interview:
  - start on time
  - maintain a pleasant but calm and impartial manner throughout
  - confirm the type of interview and explain why the interview is taking place
  - present any evidence there may be
  - invite the employee to put their side of the argument. Listen calmly and objectively and with your full attention
  - make your decision and give your reasons
  - explain to the employee that the details will remain on their file for twelve months; and that they have the right to appeal against your decision
  - explain the consequences of further misconduct etc. and state clearly how you expect the employee to behave or perform in the future
  - make a real effort to end the interview on a positive and encouraging note
- Dismissal interviews:
  - arrange for someone to counsel the employee after the dismissal interview has taken place
  - prepare a written summary of your terms for the employee, e.g. four weeks' holiday pay plus three weeks' pay in lieu of notice
  - explain your decision with apologies
  - end the interview and pass the employee on to the waiting counsellor
- Make sure the notes of the interview are typed up straight after the interview and placed securely in the employee's file.
- Most companies operate a grievance procedure in which:
  - employee states grievance, verbally or in writing, to their line manager
  - if the line manager is unable to settle the matter to the employee's satisfaction, the matter is referred to a higher authority
  - if the higher authority is unable to settle the matter to the employee's satisfaction, the matter is referred to the final authority, perhaps the MD, CEO or Board

- Redundancy represents a major life change, to which most people respond by working through a cycle of:
    - shock
    - denial
    - frustration
    - depression
    - experimentation
    - decisions
    - integration
- A redundancy plan should contain details of:
    - number of staff to be lost
    - current work location of those staff
    - start and finish dates for the redundancy programme
    - details of how all interested parties are to be informed about the arrangements
    - information regarding the financial packages to be made available
    - details of how staff are to be informed as to how they will personally be affected
- Dismissal for redundancy is deemed to be fair if:
    - the redundancy is genuine
    - the people who are to be lost have been chosen using agreed criteria
    - there is no suitable alternative work available within the company
    - selection for redundancy does not contravene the Sex or Racial Discrimination Acts.

Notes

1 Adapted from *A Handbook of Personnel Management Practice* by Michael Armstrong, Kogan Page, 4th edition (1994), p. 808.

2 Adapted from *Managing People* by Rosemary Thomson, Institute of Management/Butterworth-Heinemann (1993), p. 133.

Section 3 Counselling and support

Introduction

Even though you may never have received counselling yourself (and so may be unfamiliar with the process), there will be occasions, at work, when you will have step into a counselling role. You may need to counsel newly appointed or freshly promoted people, or those with whom you have previously had a long and untroubled relationship.

How to know when counselling is called for? When people consistently turn in poor work performance; when people who were previously competent suddenly seem unable to keep on top of the job; when people begin to behave in uncharacteristic ways – for example, excessive absenteeism or repeated and disturbing mood changes.

The purpose of counselling is to find out what is causing the problem and then help the other person to decide, for themselves, what they are going to do to put matters right. This process is often easier said than done and, occasionally, the situation will be well beyond your capabilities. If you feel out of your depth and unable to cope, it really is important that you refer the member of staff on to a trained professional. Most situations, though, simply require a non-judgemental, listening ear and a measure of ongoing support.

In this section of the workbook we'll be looking at how you can best provide workplace counselling to help people cope with the most common difficulties which usually result from the stresses of day-to-day living.

Incompetence or stress?

Everyone makes mistakes and, for most people, the first few days in a new job are very stressful. So people are much more likely to make errors and do things which, once they have settled in, they are unlikely to repeat. At the beginning, make allowances and give people some time and space to adjust.

Providing everyone is clear about what is required and what is supposed to happen, most teething problems should sort themselves out fairly quickly.

Once the 'honeymoon period' is over (when the employee has had the opportunity to settle in and get to 'know the ropes'), if you have any concerns about competence it is your responsibility to take action.

The only real way to prove incompetence is to compare **actual** performance against **expected** performance. It is therefore very important that everyone – staff and managers – knows the standards for the job. Employees should be given very clear guidelines regarding:

- what they are supposed to do
- how they are supposed to do it
- the standard to which they are supposed to do it

If you feel that someone is not meeting the standards, no matter how busy you are, don't be tempted to allow things to slide in the hope that they will improve, in time, on their own. They probably won't get better, and may get much worse.

ACTIVITY 1

Sheila, a customer service manager, explains:

'I employed a new secretary who – on her CV – seemed to have all the skills and experience needed for the job. Within a few days it became apparent that, although she was terrific on the 'phone and face-to-face with people, her keyboard and admin skills were poor, to say the least. I didn't say or do anything because I felt that it was right to let her get used to working in a new environment with new people, and new equipment. I made a big mistake ... things went from bad to worse. Her letters were poorly presented and frequently went out late, her reports were unbelievable, and the filing system was in a shambles. When my diary actually disappeared for a week I realized I had to do something ... and when I spoke to her the response was 'Well, you never said anything before.' I had to spell out exactly what I needed from her so she knew what I expected her to achieve. Things didn't get better and luckily, within a fairly short space of time, she left for another job. It was a very difficult and trying few weeks and, just before she left, I was going to start formal disciplinary action. I know, in retrospect, that I have to take responsibility for what happened and admit that I didn't manage the situation very well at all.'

Poor work performance can arise with:

- someone who is a fairly new member of staff and can, perhaps, cause you to wonder whether you have a major recruitment mistake
- someone who has been, up until now, a competent and highly valued team member

The next activity will give you an opportunity to think about how you could tackle the situation with both a new member of staff and someone who has been with the organization for a long time.

ACTIVITY 17

Read through the two case studies below and then identify questions that would help to decide what actions would be most appropriate.

Case study 1

You have recruited and selected a new member of staff who reports directly to you. Mike is employed to manage internal information and, at the interview, you were led to believe that he possessed the qualifications, skills, knowledge and experience which would enable him to perform the job to the required standard.

During his first few weeks in the job Mike makes a couple of quite serious mistakes and there are one or two complaints from your colleagues in other functions. You take the view that he is still settling in and, although you mention the problems to him and receive assurances that 'everything is under control', there is little actual improvement in performance.

After two months in the job it is apparent that Mike is not coping well and that the situation, rather than improving, is in fact deteriorating.

What would you do?

Case study 2

Ann has been with the company for almost eight years. She originally joined the organization as a secretary and immediately impressed everyone with her efficiency, hard work and ability to create good relationships with other team members and customers.

After two years she studied for and gained an IPD qualification and moved over to the Human Resource function in the role of HR co-ordinator. Four years later Ann was promoted to deputy HR manager.

Her work is consistent, competent and highly respected – until, for no apparent reason, she begins to take excessive amounts of sick leave and unauthorized absence. During her last period off work, a colleague discovers discrepancies in her paperwork; tasks left uncompleted; staff issues that have not been actioned; redundancy payments that have been incorrectly calculated and paid.

What would you do?

FEEDBACK

Case Study 1

You would have to use your judgement, consider the following questions and answer them **honestly**:

- Does Mike really understand what he is supposed to do, how he is supposed to do it, and to what standard?
- Is Mike genuinely incompetent or are there other reasons why things have gone wrong? e.g. Is he still adapting to working in a new environment? Does he have pressing personal problems? Is he receiving an acceptable level of support from colleagues? Are these mistakes due to his incompetence, or are they due to something or someone else? Is he covering for someone else?
- Have I monitored Mike's work sufficiently well, or have I walked away, and left him to get on with it? As Mike's line manager, how much of the problem is, in fact, **my** responsibility? Is there anything I should have done – or could do in the future – to ensure that things improve?

Case study 2

You would have to use your judgement, consider the following questions and answer them **honestly**:

- Has Ann been promoted without being given the benefit of appropriate, ongoing training? Has she been overloaded with responsibility? Are the absences due to work-related stress? Or, does she have a physical illness about which nobody at work has thought to enquire?

- Does Ann have pressing personal problems which she has not felt able to discuss with anyone at work?

- Have I (and her colleagues) given her sufficient support and encouragement?

- As her line manager, to what extent is this problem **my** responsibility? Have I contributed in any way to the current situation?

Having thought your way through these questions, in both cases, your next step should be to arrange an informal, one-to-one counselling meeting with Mike and with Ann to find out more.

The counselling process

There are many different forms of counselling, many of which need to be undertaken by trained and experienced practitioners. The next activity will give you an opportunity to think about how you interpret the term *counselling*.

ACTIVITY 18

Please complete the following sentence:
I think that counselling involves

FEEDBACK

Counselling is a process which takes place between two people: the counsellor and the client. The process involves the counsellor giving to the client:

- time
- attention
- respect

so as to allow the client to explore (with the counsellor) a personal problem – or problems – and, hopefully, identify possible solutions.

More and more, managers are finding themselves responsible for counselling team members at work. This is fine, up to a point. But it is important to remember that competent counselling requires a range of skills, knowledge and specific techniques, all of which should be supported by appropriate training and, ideally, considerable experience.

There is no reason why an untrained counsellor should not **begin** the process. In many cases, someone may simply need an attentive listening ear, time to unburden themselves and a little honest support and encouragement. Sometimes, though, starting the counselling process can uncover serious problems with which the untrained counsellor is simply not equipped to deal.

A specially trained Relate, Samaritan, Alcohol Anonymous or NHS counsellor would be necessary to provide a full range of support to someone experiencing:

- severe relationship and sexuality problems
- clinical depression, thoughts of suicide or a specific, recognized mental illness such as schizophrenia or manic-depression
- a terminal life-threatening disease
- continuous, uncontrollable substance abuse

Your role as a workplace counsellor is to ask the right questions, listen a great deal, and then either:

- help the client (the person sitting in the other chair) to identify some practical steps they could take towards beginning to deal with the problem, or
- refer them to a professional with the appropriate expertise to offer the kind of counselling the client needs

The counselling interview

When a member of your team is experiencing problems at work which are evidenced by poor job performance, your first task is to set up a one-to-one interview. The purpose of this interview is to:

1   create a supportive environment for the client
2   establish rapport with the client
3   encourage the client to discuss the problem and allow the client to explore the reasons why the problem exists
4   encourage the client to identify and explore possible solutions
5   allow the client to choose their preferred solution, or refer the client to a trained counsellor

CREATING A SUPPORTIVE ENVIRONMENT

You will need a completely private space for the interview. This should be out of sight (and preferably out of hearing) of anyone else. There should **no** interruptions or distractions of any kind, and you should allow up to two hours for a counselling interview.

Welcome the member of staff pleasantly, offer them tea or coffee, seat yourself beside them, and don't perch behind your desk. That approach is totally inappropriate for this kind of interview.

Your aim should be to show your client, by what you say and do, that this is **not** a disciplinary interview. It is an informal meeting which, hopefully, will be of benefit to both of you. A serious word of caution. Don't attempt to conduct a counselling interview if you are angry, upset, exhausted or irrationally hostile to the client. It simply won't work, and could make matters worse. If you don't feel that you can give the member of staff the time, attention and respect they deserve, then ask someone else to do it for you.

ESTABLISHING RAPPORT

How you do this will depend on your own personal style, and the person in the other chair. You may want to take a few minutes to talk about a neutral topic which is of mutual interest, or you may want to get straight down to business – 'Thanks for coming to see me Ann. There are a couple of issues I'd like to explore with you and get some feedback on.'

ENCOURAGING DISCUSSION OF THE PROBLEM

The next step is to open up the conversation and get the problem out in the open. 'The main reason why I wanted to see you is that I've noticed you've been taking a considerable amount of time off work recently. You're a valued member of the team and, naturally, I'm concerned about this. What seems to be the problem?'

Ask open questions (how? why? what? where? who?) to encourage the client to talk. Listen carefully and attentively, saying as little as possible. Don't jump in, interrupt, offer advice, make suggestions or try, in two or three words, to present the perfect solution. Finding the solution is not for you to do – it is up to your client.

Where someone is experiencing difficulties, the kindest and most beneficial thing you can do, in many cases, is simply to listen.

ACTIVITY 20

What personal issues might cause someone to have difficulty with meeting the required standards of work performance?

1

2

3

4

FEEDBACK

People may turn in poor job performance for a whole host of reasons including:

- difficulties with personal relationships – breakdown, separation, divorce etc.
- difficulties with work relationships
- grief, loss and bereavement
- loss of confidence and self-esteem; emotional insecurity
- eating disorders – bulimia, anorexia nervosa
- substance abuse – alcohol, drugs
- financial difficulties – debt, house repossession, bankruptcy
- lack of appropriate training
- not being sure of what it is they are supposed to do
- being promoted beyond their capabilities

It is highly unlikely that someone is going to immediately say 'I'm sorry I'm doing such a lousy job but my wife has left me for my best friend and I'm hitting the bottle' or 'Well I started taking cocaine for a laugh, and now I'm hooked' or even 'I just don't have any confidence any more.' To get to the root of the problem you have to, patiently, ask questions and allow the client the opportunity to talk freely. If you are in any way critical or judgemental, they will say nothing. The person in the other chair will only open up if they feel they are in a supportive and encouraging situation.

Once your client has actually brought the problem into the open – 'Well, I suppose I'm just really tired all the time' or 'Yes, I know I've been really difficult to work with' it is time to probe a little to find out more. 'Why do you think you're so tired?' or 'What do you think it is that's making you difficult to work with?' may begin to edge nearer to the real problem. Don't, whatever you do, tell the client why they are tired, or why they are difficult, or why their performance is below standard. They have to tell you.

ENCOURAGING IDENTIFICATION AND EXPLORATION OF POSSIBLE SOLUTIONS

In some situations you may be able to see the problem and the solution with perfect clarity. You know what you would do; you know what you think the client should do ... it's obvious! At this point resist the temptation to share your insights. It is not the role of a counsellor to provide solutions, no matter how tempting this option might seem.

ACTIVITY 21

Why is it neither useful nor helpful for a counsellor to impose a solution?

FEEDBACK

The client must own the problem. It is their problem and they have to find the solution which is acceptable to them. Once a counsellor begins to impose suggestions – 'Well, if I were you, I'd ...' or 'Under the circumstances, I think the best thing you can do is ...' – the client loses ownership, and loses control. Where a solution is imposed, many clients will think 'Oh well, that's what I suppose I should do ...' but they will soon lose interest because they have no real commitment to the ideas, and feel as though they have no real control over the outcome.
Ask:

'What you feel is the best way to go?
'What are your ideas about this?'
'How would you prefer to tackle the problem?'

You can offer suggestions:

- 'have you thought about ...?'
- 'you might want to consider ...?'
- 'another option would be to ...?'

but always make sure that you generate a list of alternatives and offer them as options the client might want to think about, and not as your advice.

Remember, the art of good counselling involves helping people to look at a range of options and then make their own decision.

ENCOURAGING DECISION MAKING (OR REFERRING THE CLIENT TO A TRAINED COUNSELLOR)

The last stage of the interview is about helping the client to choose the preferred option. You may have to write down, on a piece of paper, all the pros and cons for all the options. Or spell out the advantages and disadvantages. Or even sit in silence for ten minutes while the client mulls it over.

The key points here are:

- do not impose your preferred solution
- if you feel the problem is too serious for you to manage on your own, do not hesitate to refer the client to a professional, trained counsellor

CLOSING THE INTERVIEW

Depending on the client, the problem and the circumstances they may feel lots better, while you may feel much, much worse than when you started. They may feel better because they have:

- unburdened themselves
- been listened to
- identified the root of the problem and the cause of the problem (and this may be new information for them)
- found a possible solution

You may feel worse because you have expended a great deal of time and energy, or because the matter is far more serious than you originally thought, and you have not been able to help as much as you originally hoped.

It is your job, as the counsellor, to gently draw the interview to a close. You can do this by summarizing the decision and, where appropriate, agreements which have been made during the meeting. For example:

'OK Mike, I think we've agreed the next step is for me to arrange a training day for you so that you can really familiarize yourself with the TGK software. I'll also arrange for Susan to spend time with you next week going through your job description, just to clarify any additional areas where extra training might be useful.'

'OK Ann, I think we're agreed that you need some additional help. And I think we're both clear that Relate are the people who are best qualified to help. You said you would ring tomorrow and set up an appointment – yes?'

Finally, always set the date for the next meeting. This is important because you need to:

- check that agreed actions have been carried out
- identify improvements or additional steps which need to be taken to resolve the situation
- confirm to the person in the other chair that you **are** interested and that you **will be** monitoring the situation

Finally, never, ever betray a confidence which has been disclosed during a counselling interview except with the express permission of the client. You may have to ask for this – 'Ann this is clearly such a serious matter that I need to discuss the implications with Helen. I need your permission to do that, so is it OK with you?' Failure to maintain confidence is unethical, unprofessional and will reflect on you, as a manager and an individual.

Use the next activity as an opportunity to check out your counselling responses in a range of situations.

ACTIVITY 21

Read through the following four scenarios and select, from the options given, what you consider to be the one most appropriate response for each.

1 During the counselling interview **Claire** bursts into tears and discloses that her poor work performance is because her husband recently lost his job. He is now spending his days in the pub and the betting shop and she is deeply worried about both the marriage, and their financial situation. How would you respond?

   a 'Well Claire, you're going to have to pull yourself together aren't you?' ❑

   b 'Whatever you do, you mustn't let it get you down. Just get on with your job and I'm sure things will sort themselves out.' ❑

   c 'Sounds terrible to me – I definitely wouldn't put up with that. ❑

   d 'What do you think is preventing your husband from looking for work?' ❑

2 **Peter** is a widower in his thirties. During the counselling interview he discloses he has three young children at home and he has just been diagnosed as an insulin-dependant diabetic. How would you respond?

   a 'Well, it seems to me as though you've got too much on your plate at the moment.' ❑

   b 'What kind of changes could we make here to help you adjust to this new situation? ❑

   c 'If I were you I'd find out if there some other kind of treatment apart from injections ... how would you feel about that?' ❑

   d 'It's not the end of the world. Don't you think you're over-reacting?' ❑

3 **Sam** discloses that he is finding his recent promotion to team leader, at the age of fifty-four, extremely stressful. How would you respond?

   a 'Stick it out Sam. It's not that long to retirement and it'll make a big difference to your pension.' ❑

   b 'If I were you I'd go back to the shop floor – I don't think any job is worth that much stress.' ❑

   c 'What would make it easier for you to cope with the job?' ❑

   d 'It's not too late to change your mind you know – but have you thought about the future?' ❑

4 **Tony** discloses during the counselling interview that he has been feeling ill for some time and is terrified that he may be HIV positive. How would you respond?

   a 'If I were you I'd take a test straight away – that way you'll know, one way or another.' ❑

   b 'What makes you think you're at risk?' ❑

c 'Well first of all, I wouldn't tell anyone else. Secondly I'd go to see my doctor.' ❏

d 'How would you feel about looking at all the possible options? ❏

FEEDBACK

The most helpful responses, in each of these situations, would be:

1 Claire: option 4 'What do you think is preventing your husband from looking for work?' This response gives Claire the opportunity to explore some possibilities to which she may not have given her attention previously.

2 Peter: option 2 'What kind of changes could we make here to help you adjust to this new situation?' This response gives Peter the opportunity to think about, and to say, what would help him most.

3 Sam: option 3 'What would make it easy for you to cope with the job?' This response gives Sam the opportunity to ask for help, advice, assistance – whatever he thinks might be useful – without appearing incompetent.

4 Tony: option 4 'How would you feel about looking at all the possible options?' This response gives Tony an opportunity to consider the options and then to look at all the alternatives and, perhaps with the counsellor's assistance, draw up a checklist of benefits and disadvantages for each possibility.

All the other responses given are either judgmental or directive, and so are neither helpful or useful.

Counselling isn't easy and it isn't a quick fix. Some people may need four or five or even more counselling interviews because you, the counsellor, are their only support. Some people may sort themselves out after a couple of meetings, take the agreed action, solve the problem and never look back. Some people may improve for a little while and then slide back again. Some problems, like serious drug abuse for example, may need much more attention than a few workplace counselling sessions. Everyone is different, and has different needs. The key point to remember is that, if you are not a qualified counsellor, you may need to refer people on.

Summary

- Counselling may be appropriate for staff who:
    - appear to be having difficulties meeting normal work standards
    - begin to behave in uncharacteristic ways
    - take excessive amounts of sick leave or unauthorized absence
- The purpose of counselling is to give someone the opportunity to explore the reasons why they are having difficulties and give them the time, space and appropriate support to enable them to discover their own solutions.
- Anyone who takes on a counselling role must be prepared to give the client:
    - time
    - attention
    - respect
- It is not the job of the counsellor to suggest or impose solutions.
- The structure of a counselling interview should be:
    - establish rapport
    - encourage the client to disclose and discuss the problem
    - allow the client to explore the reason why the problem exists
    - encourage the client to identify and explore possible solutions
    - allow the client to choose their preferred solution
    - gently draw the meeting to a close by summarizing what has been discussed and the steps (if any) the client plans to take to ease the situation and solve the problem
    - agree a date for another meeting
    - **never** betray a confidence which has been disclosed during a counselling interview UNLESS you have the client's express permission
- It is of paramount importance that workplace counsellors recognize when clients need professional counselling help. **Never** resist referring someone on to a professional.

Section 4 Health and safety

Introduction

The health and safety of employees (plus customers, suppliers and visitors to premises) is a key management issue. Managers need to be able to take:

1 A **strategic** approach which looks at how, in the long term, the organization should be managing health and safety
2 A **pro-active** approach which looks at how health and safety matters can be managed effectively on a day-to-day basis
3 A **personal** approach which looks at how managers can, through their individual actions and responses, take a measure of personal responsibility for promoting and ensuring health and safety throughout the organization

In this section of the workbook we'll be looking at these three approaches to managing and implementing sound health and safety practices at work.

A strategic approach to health and safety

The main purposes of health and safety laws and regulations are to ensure that people have a safe and healthy working environment and that, as far as possible, accidents can be prevented. An accident can reasonably be described as 'an event that results in harm or damage to people or property or causes loss or disruption to process or procedures'.
The main current legislation is:

- Management of Health & Safety at Work Regulations 1992
- Workplace (Health, Safety & Welfare) Regulations 1992 (often referred to as the Workplace Regulations)
- Manual Handling Operations Regulations 1992
- Health and Safety (Display Screen Equipment) Regulations 1992
- Personal Protective Equipment at Work Regulations 1992
- Control of Substances Hazardous to Health (1988)
- Health & Safety at Work etc. Act 1974 (often referred to as HASAWA)

- Factories Act 1961 (which will eventually be completely superseded by the 1992 Regulations – see below)
- Offices, Shops & Railway Premises Act 1963

Under this legislation employers have a legal duty of care towards their employees, customers, suppliers and visitors. In practice, this means that employers are required to provide a safe and healthy working environment, and also to make sure that the services they provide or the products they make are safe.

Effective health and safety – safe workplace, safe working practices, safe equipment and so on – has to be influenced top-down throughout the organization. In other words, once the staff know what is required of them it is their responsibility to do it, but it has to be the responsibility of senior management to develop health and safety policies and programmes, and make sure that these are effective.

ACTIVITY 22

For the purpose of this activity imagine that you are a member of the senior management within a completely new business. The MD asks you to 'Create a health and safety management programme to make sure that, when we open, everything to do with health and safety is as it should be.'

What do you think are some of the key steps and considerations in meeting this requirement?

FEEDBACK

The nine key steps for senior management, when creating a health and safety management programme are:

1 **analyse** the premises and working practices and identify the potential problems
2 **develop** health and safety policies and procedures
3 **organize** health and safety personnel and allocate individual responsibilities
4 **arrange** appropriate training
5 **devise** appropriate documentation
6 **implement** policies and procedures
7 **undertake** inspections and audits
8 **evaluate** performance
9 **make** changes and improvements, where necessary

ANALYSING THE PREMISES AND WORKING PRACTICES AND IDENTIFYING THE POTENTIAL PROBLEMS

This step involves taking an in-depth look at every part of the building to make sure that it is safe. This includes everything from the structure and fabric of the building right down to identifying torn carpeting, spaghetti-junctions of electric cable, boxes of stationery dumped in the hallway, step ladders draped against the exit door, fire extinguishers that don't work and first-aid boxes that contain nothing more than two safety pins and an out-of-date sticking plaster.

It also means making sure that every single item of equipment (in the offices, warehouse, factory floor and on the road) is safe to use and regularly checked and serviced by someone who is suitably qualified and trained to do the checking. This includes ensuring that old, out-of-date and possibly unsafe plant, machinery and equipment is replaced with new (and possibly expensive) alternatives. Health and safety law is not interested in cash-flow problems or impressed by comments like 'I was waiting to get the latest model which comes on the market next year.' If someone is harmed at work by unsafe equipment, then the employer is responsible.

It also includes making sure that everything from the layout of the building to the way in which production processes are organized and arranged should be safe for people. So, for example, it could be argued that it is unsafe to have the main reception desk sited right next to the ornamental fountain – on the basis that water and electricity (needed for the computer) are not a safe combination. It would be expected that a laboratory process involving radiation or acid or bacteria should be shielded from the rest of the building, and it would be reasonable to ensure that someone who regularly moves trays of hot material should not be expected to walk between two rows of desks where people are writing reports and making telephone calls.

And it also means that no one should be at risk of hurting themselves at work because they have to carry or move something which is too heavy, too large or toxic. This is not just obviously heavy objects like crates and pallets, but also smaller items such as printers and boxes of photocopying paper.

So this first stage of analysis involves identifying all of the potential risks, plus all the health and safety equipment and peripheral items needed. These might include anything from trolleys for moving heavy items through to protective clothing; fire extinguishers through to 'Exit' and 'No Smoking' signs.

DEVELOPING HEALTH AND SAFETY POLICIES AND PROCEDURES

This involves developing the procedures to be carried out in respect of:

- accident handling, investigation, reporting and documentation
- fire prevention and fire handling
- carrying out checks and inspections on the company's buildings, plant, equipment and machinery
- carrying out checks and inspections on health and safety equipment such as fire extinguishers, first-aid boxes, goggles, footwear and so on
- preventing and, where necessary, monitoring potentially harmful emissions from working practices
- monitoring good housekeeping practices such as storage facilities, waste disposal, safe use of machinery, electricity and gas
- ensuring that all health and safety matters are up to date and comply with current legislation

ORGANIZING HEALTH AND SAFETY PERSONNEL AND ALLOCATING INDIVIDUAL RESPONSIBILITIES

Once you are clear about the procedures you need to adopt, then you need to identify the people who will be responsible for making sure that the procedures are actually carried out. (In any company with more than five employees, a manager must be appointed and trained as the company's Safety Representative.) The number of people and their individual responsibilities will depend on the type and size of the organization. Two possible structures are shown in Figures 7 and 8.

Two Owners/Partners
with equally shared ultimate responsibility for health and safety

Office Manager (designated and trained Safety Representative)
with responsibility for making sure that all health and safety procedures
are implemented and that legislation is complied with in all respects

Senior Secretary
who is a trained first-aid provider

Figure 7   Health and safety structure for a small service company employing eight people

ARRANGING APPROPRIATE TRAINING

Everyone in the company, from the Managing Director through to the person responsible for taking care of the dish-washing machine in the canteen kitchen, must have adequate and appropriate health and safety training. This should include training in:

- hazard identification and reporting
- accident, illness, fire and explosion prevention and reporting
- building evacuation, including location of exits, entrances and fire extinguishers; escape routes and procedures
- safe working practices, including hygiene and good housekeeping
- safe operation of plant, machinery and equipment, including use of protective clothing and equipment, and the servicing and maintenance schedules for machinery
- safe handling of substances hazardous to health
- first-aid procedures and obtaining medical assistance, including location of first-aid boxes, first-aid room and first-aid personnel
- names and locations of health and safety officers, representatives and other trained personnel

Everyone should know which machines they are and are not allowed to use. **Everyone** should be adequately trained to use their permitted machinery and equipment. This applies not only to recognized potentially dangerous items like fork-lift trucks, band saws and drills, but also to items like electric staplers, photocopy machines, computers and even craft knives. If an employee injures themselves and truthfully says 'I was never told I had to take the plug out before I put my hand in' it is the employer's responsibility. The key point here is that people should know what to do and how to do it both to prevent accidents and problems, and to deal with accidents or problems when they occur.

Chairman and Board of Directors with equally shared ultimate responsibility for health & safety

↓

Director of Human Resources with responsibility for making sure that all health & safety procedures are implemented and that legislation is complied with in all respects

↓

Human Resources Manager responsible for devising health & safety procedures and documentation, and the recruitment and selection of health & safety personnel	Training and Development Manager responsible for devising training material, and for the training and updating of all health & safety personnel

↓

Health & Safety Officer with responsibility for ensuring health & safety procedures are adhered to	Health & Safety Officer with responsibility for ensuring health & safety procedures are adhered to	Health & Safety Officer with responsibility for ensuring health & safety procedures are adhered to	Health & Safety Officer with responsibility for ensuring health & safety procedures are adhered to

↓

Departmental Managers responsible for ensuring health & safety in their own department	Departmental Managers responsible for ensuring health & safety in their own department	Departmental Managers responsible for ensuring health & safety in their own department	Departmental Managers responsible for ensuring health & safety in their own department	Departmental Managers responsible for ensuring health & safety in their own department

↓

Health & Safety Team Leader	Health & Safety Team Leader	Health & Safety Team Leader	Health & Safety Team Leader	Health & Safety Team Leader	Health & Safety Team Leader

↓

Trained First-aid Provider	Trained First-aid Provider	Trained First-aid Provider	Trained First-aid Provider

Health & Safety Fire Warden	Health & Safety Fire Warden	Health & Safety Fire Warden	Health & Safety Fire Warden	Health & Safety Fire Warden	Health & Safety Fire Warden

Figure 8   Health and safety structure for a large manufacturing company employing 350 people

DEVISING APPROPRIATE DOCUMENTATION

Health and safety documentation includes:

- information packs for staff (including updates when new legislation appears)

- accident report, investigation and conclusion forms
- equipment inspection and maintenance forms
- first-aid treatment and patient progress forms
- fire drill forms
- health and safety audit forms
- health and safety statistic forms (detailing the number of accidents, fires and so on)

IMPLEMENTING POLICIES AND PROCEDURES

It isn't the end of the story when all the policies, procedures and documentation are in place, and everyone has had the training. This is when people – managers, health and safety officers, team leaders – have to make sure that they drive the programme through and that staff are sticking to the procedures, and the procedures work in the way they were intended to work.

As a manager, no matter what your key objectives are, or what your particular specialism or area of interest, health and safety has to be high on your agenda. The legislation which governs and controls health and safety in the UK is very clear that it is the **employer's responsibility** to make sure the staff are working in a healthy and safe environment. This means that, as part of the management team, you have to keep your eye on the ball and never, ever dismiss any aspect of health and safety as something that is just the 'flavour of the month' or 'an intrusion on the real business we're here for'. Specifically, if you see something which needs attention (even if it is a minor problem like a pile of rubbish, or a Fire Exit sign that is hanging off the wall), don't walk by because you are too busy dealing with profit and loss, or productivity or market share. No company wants to have staff injuries or deaths on its conscience, and no company can afford the bad press which always accompanies a bad safety record. So, from both an ethical and a purely commercial point of view, good health and safety awareness and practices make sound business sense.

UNDERTAKING INSPECTIONS AND AUDITS

Safety inspections and audits play a key role in raising health and safety awareness within an organization. They also ensure that all the equipment, systems and procedures are properly maintained and servicing is recorded.

EVALUATING PERFORMANCE

By looking at the results of the inspections and audits you can see, from the figures, whether or not the company's health and safety performance is adequate, good or outstanding.

MAKING CHANGES AND IMPROVEMENTS, WHERE NECESSARY

Depending on the evaluation of performance it may be necessary to make changes and improvements. These changes may include:

- implementing additional procedures
- changing existing procedures or documentation
- changing some elements of the health and safety training programme
- appointing additional staff to take responsibility for health and safety

The next activity will give you an opportunity to consider some of these issues, and may help to provide evidence for Element A2.4.

ACTIVITY 23   A2.2, A3.3

Think about the way in which health and safety is managed and implemented within your own organization. See if you can identify, for each of the topics listed below, improvements or changes which would be of benefit to both the company and the employees.

1   Analysis of the premises and working practices, and identification of potential problems.
    How, in your opinion, could this process be improved?

2   Development of health and safety procedures.
    Are there any procedures which could be improved? How could these improvements be implemented?

3   Organization of health and safety personnel, and allocation of individual responsibilities.
    Does the current health and safety personnel structure work? Is the way in which responsibilities are allocated effective and appropriate? Do you have any suggestions for improvement?

4   Appropriate training.
    Is current health and safety training appropriate and sufficient for everyone? Could you suggest how training might be improved?

5   Appropriate documentation.

    Is the current documentation straightforward and easy to use? What changes
    could you suggest for improvement?

6   Implementation of policies and procedures.

    Are there any ways in which health and safety procedures in your organization
    could be sharpened up and improved?

7   Inspections and audits.

    Are inspections and audits undertaken regularly, and thoroughly? How might
    these be improved?

8   Evaluation of performance.

    How is the evaluation of performance undertaken, and who is responsible? Do
    you have any suggestions for improvement?

9   Making changes and improvements.

    Is your organization responsive to the evaluation results? Are changes and
    improvements actually carried out, when necessary? What would you do to
    improve the process?

A pro-active approach to health and safety

Every organization has to make sure that it is complying with the legal and
regulatory health and safety requirements. This compliance has to be consistent, appropriate and monitored on a daily or even hourly basis (where, say,
excessive amounts of waste material are generated).

Taking a pro-active approach to health and safety means that, as a
manager, working for any kind of organization, anywhere in the UK, you need
to know both the law and the regulations, so you can:

■   judge whether or not the law and the regulations are being complied with
■   know what to do to put things right, when necessary

WORKPLACE REGULATIONS

The 1992 Workplace Regulations are a key item of European legislation and relevant to most workplaces.

ACTIVITY 24

List six hygiene, welfare or environmental issues that are covered by current legislation and which you, as a manager, need to be aware of.

1
2
3
4
5
6

FEEDBACK

The main health and safety issues covered by the 1992 Workplace Regulations (in alphabetical order, **not** in order of importance) are:

- cleanliness and waste
- conditions of floors or traffic routes
- drinking water
- escalators and moving walkways
- facilities for storing and changing clothes
- falls or falling objects
- indoor temperatures
- lighting
- maintenance of equipment and systems
- rest period accommodation and meal facilities
- room dimensions and space
- sanitary and washing facilities
- seating and workstations
- ventilation
- windows, gates, walls and doors

(For additional information see Section 5 of this workbook.)

COSHH

Under the Control of Substances Hazardous to Health (COSHH) Regulations 1988 organizations are required to:

■ identify and assess the risks to health
■ decide on the necessary precautions
■ control or prevent the risks
■ ensure the control measures are continuously implemented
■ monitor the exposure to risk and, where necessary, the health of employees
■ ensure that employees are informed of the risks, and trained to avoid and prevent them

To identify substances hazardous to health you can check Part IA1 of the Approved List, Classification, Packaging and Labelling of Dangerous Substances Regulations 1984. Any substances listed there as very toxic, toxic, corrosive, harmful or irritant are covered by the COSHH regulations.

Aside from specific substances (corrosives, acids, solvents etc.) that are used for a specific purpose, it is also useful to think about production processes to identify whether staff might be at risk from dust, fumes or residues. It is worth noting that asbestos, lead and radio-active materials all have their own specific handling regulations which must be complied with.

HASAWA

The Health & Safety at Work Act 1974 is the **key** piece of legislation which applies, in its entirety, to **every** company in the UK. The next activity will give you an opportunity to consider what this really means, in practical terms.

ACTIVITY 25

Under the Health & Safety at Work Act 1974:

1 For whose health and safety is an employer responsible?

2 For whose health and safety is an employee responsible?

Under HASAWA, **employers** are responsible for the health and safety of:

- employees and other workers, whether they are:
    - full time or part-time
    - permanent, temporary or casual
    - on work experience from school or college
    - attending the workplace as part of a Government training scheme
- visitors:
    - on site as a subcontractor
    - visiting or using the premises for any purpose
    - using the firm's equipment for any purpose
- customers buying or using products made, or services supplied, by the organization
- members of the general public, particularly those living in the local neighbourhood near to the workplace who might be affected by noise, toxic emissions and so on

Basically, this list covers just about **anyone** who works at or visits the workplace, for whatever reason.

Under Section 7(a) of HASAWA, **employees'** health and safety responsibilities are defined as:

It shall be the duty of every employee while at work to take reasonable care for the health and safety of himself and of other persons who may be affected by his acts or omissions at work.

In practice, this means that each employee is responsible for their own health and safety, and the health and safety of everyone who works at or visits the workplace premises.

FINANCIAL IMPLICATIONS

As we said earlier, ethics dictate that companies should comply with the legislation. In addition, compliance is good business practice because the financial implications of health and safety problems can be considerable.

ACTIVITY 26

For the purposes of this activity imagine that, in your organization, two employees, whilst operating machinery, are involved in a serious accident. Both employees are hospitalized and need to be off work for at least three months each. List four of the likely financial costs your company would have to meet as a result of the accident.

1

2

3

4

FEEDBACK

The financial implications of a serious accident involving two employees could include the cost of:

- sickness benefit and/or compensation for the individuals involved in the accident
- additional payments to replacement staff – agency people or overtime payments to existing employees
- lost production or reduced service levels
- repair or replacement of damaged or faulty machinery
- accident investigation and reporting procedures
- management meetings to discuss future accident prevention measures to be implemented
- increased premium to insurance company (although research figures show that over 90 per cent of the financial costs of a workplace accident are uninsured)
- bad press, possibly accompanied by loss of consumer and shareholder confidence, maybe resulting in:
    - loss of market share
    - reduction in share prices
    - loss of future investment or loan facilities

Apart from accidents, unsafe or unacceptable working practices can also cause considerable financial loss. This has been shown to be the case during the adverse publicity surrounding the BSE Mad Cow controversy. Some companies immediately swung into action to reassure the public that their working practices were being totally overhauled and updated. For those companies public confidence remained strong, and they retained their market share. Other companies decided that it was 'a fuss about nothing which would quickly blow over'. UK consumers retaliated by reducing their purchases of British beef and disassociating themselves from companies which had not strictly followed the health and safety guidelines relating to slaughter and carcass stripping. The public voted with their feet, and their money.

There would also be other equally important costs which may not necessarily be financial. These could include:

■ loss of employee confidence
■ reduction in employee motivation and morale, possibly accompanied by lowered productivity or quality standards

The key point here is that once the strategic, long-term planning has been done, and all the staff, systems and procedures are in place, every company must take a pro-active, even aggressive, approach to health and safety. This means keeping up to date with and conforming to the legislation; regularly updating and improving staff training; constantly monitoring and persistently looking at ways in which continuous health and safety improvements can be made. Health and safety should never be just a paper exercise. Get it wrong, and you put families, careers, even lives at risk.

A personal approach to health and safety

As a manager, you have health and safety responsibilities towards:

■ your employer
■ your colleagues
■ your team
■ anyone and everyone who visits your company's premises, or who uses your company's products or services
■ yourself

ACTIVITY 27

How can you, at a personal level, make a practical contribution to health and safety at work? List three things you can do to demonstrate your personal commitment to health and safety.

1

2

3

FEEDBACK

Whether you like it or not, you are a role model for excellence. In matters of health and safety (and most other things too) you have to lead from the front and set a good example.

CASE STUDY

David, an accountant, and member of his company's senior management team, describes how he learned the hard way about example setting:

'We were in Scotland in the middle of winter and I'd spent three hours on-site talking to people. As you can imagine, I was absolutely frozen. I was on my way back to my car and, to be honest, all I could think about was whether or not I was ever going to be able to defrost my feet. Then I realized I'd forgotten to give a really important instruction to the site foreman ... so I popped back, just wanting to get the whole thing over with as quickly as possible. I didn't call back into the main building for the protective gear ... well, I was only going to be there for a minute, wasn't I? Long story cut short ... there was a problem with one of the cranes and I missed instant death by about 2 cm. No one congratulated me on living to tell the tale ... but there was a great deal of bad feeling because I was on-site without a hard hat. That story ran and ran ... and I was very disadvantaged by it. I couldn't take anyone to task about health and safety at work ... because everyone felt that if I had no respect for the rules, why should they bother?'

The practical things you can do to demonstrate personal commitment to health and safety are:

- Lead from the front
  - observe the rules and regulations at all times
  - take appropriate action when you see other people who are not observing the rules. Don't just walk past and turn a blind eye
  - listen carefully to problems, concerns and suggestions for improvement, and then take appropriate action
  - say nothing and do nothing **ever** which might give people the impression that you do not regard health and safety as a key issue, of paramount importance
- Check and monitor, constantly
  - walk the job and see for yourself whether or not everything is in order; whether or not people are observing health and safety requirements
  - always make it known that you are serious about the topic and that you expect other people to be serious, too

Summary

- A **strategic approach** involves looking at how the organization should be managing health and safety in the long term
- A **pro-active approach** involves looking at how health and safety can be managed on a day-to-day basis
- A **personal approach** involves taking personal responsibility for ensuring the promotion and observance of health and safety practices and procedures
- The nine key steps for creating a health and safety management programme are:
    - 1 analyse the situation and identify potential problems
    - 2 develop policies and procedures
    - 3 organize personnel and allocate responsibilities
    - 4 arrange training
    - 5 devise documentation
    - 6 implement systems, policies and procedures
    - 7 undertake inspections and audits
    - 8 evaluate performance
    - 9 make any necessary changes
- The main pieces of legislation which you, as a manager, need to be familiar with are:
    - The Management of Health & Safety at Work Regulations 1992
    - Workplace (Health, Safety & Welfare) Regulations 1992
    - Control of Substances Hazardous to Health Regulations 1988 (COSHH)
    - Health & Safety at Work etc. Act 1974 (HASAWA)
- As a manager you can demonstrate personal commitment to health and safety by:
    - observing the rules **all the time**
    - taking action when you see others who are not observing the rules
    - listening carefully to health and safety concerns – and take action to put things right
    - walking the job and seeing for yourself what is going on
    - letting everyone know that you are serious about health and safety – and that you expect people to follow the rules

Section 5　The law

Introduction

Anyone involved in recruiting, selecting and appointing employees must tread very carefully to ensure that the law is carefully observed throughout each stage of the process. And everyone at work has some responsibility for health and safety.

In this final section of the workbook we will be looking at the most important legislation which, as a manager, you need to be familiar with.

Recruitment and the law

JOB ADVERTISING AND THE LAW

Job advertisements must comply with the:

- Code of Practice of the Council for Racial Equality
- Code of Practice of the Equal Opportunities Commission

This means that advertisements must not contain any sexist or racist implications, e.g. 'Women over 40 need not apply'.

Discrimination is **only** allowed where race or gender (male/female) is a genuine occupational requirement:

- if the job specifically requires a man or a woman for reasons of privacy, e.g. Lavatory Attendant or Bathing & Dressing Attendant in a nursing home
- if the job is residential and **only** single-sex sleeping and toilet accommodation are available
- if the job involves modelling clothes or playing a part in a film, TV, stage or radio production
- if the job requires the services of a married couple, e.g. residential housekeeper and gardener to share a flat or cottage provided as part of the remuneration
- if the job involves working abroad in a country where the customs and practices of the country would prevent someone of a particular race or gender from carrying out their job duties

APPLICATION FORMS AND THE LAW

Job Applications Forms must **not** ask candidates to:

- disclose information about their marital status, dependants, ethnic origins, race, religion, sexual preference and so on (Racial Equality and Equal Opportunities Codes of Practice)
- provide information about union membership, (this is covered under Trade Union and Labour Relations legislation)
- disclose information regarding a previous served prison sentence unless the vacancy is for:
    - an accountant or similar professional
    - someone to provide supervision or training for young people
    - someone to look after elderly, sick or disabled people

EQUAL OPPORTUNITIES MONITORING POLICY AND THE LAW

If your company is implementing a formal equal opportunities monitoring policy then, and only then, is it possible to ask candidates to provide information about their gender and/or ethnic group. Under these circumstances, it is acceptable to state on the application form something along the lines of:

As part of our Equal Opportunities Monitoring Policy we would ask you to tick the relevant boxes which apply to you. The information you provide will enable us to eliminate discrimination on the grounds of race, colour, sex or marital status. Whilst this information will only be used for monitoring purposes and will be kept strictly confidential, if these boxes are left blank this will not in any way affect your application.

INTERVIEW QUESTIONS ABOUT PAST CONVICTIONS AND THE LAW[1]

The Rehabilitation of Offenders Act 1974 allows some criminal convictions to become 'spent' after a certain period of time. This means that:

1. the person is not required to disclose a 'spent' conviction to a prospective employer
2. the person should be treated as if they have not been convicted of a criminal offence

A candidate who has a spent conviction is not obliged to reveal this information at interview.

- 'Spent' convictions: A prison or corrective training sentence of **between six and thirty months** becomes spent after ten years.
- A prison or corrective training sentence of **more than thirty months** can never be regarded as spent.

There are a number of 'excluded professions' such as teaching and nursing, and someone applying for an 'excluded profession' vacancy is:

1   under a statutory obligation to disclose the conviction, even if it is 'spent'
2   excluded from the normal protection

REFERENCES AND THE LAW

People looking for jobs in the finance sector and covered by Lautro or Fimbra regulations are required to provide references. Otherwise, there is no obligation to provide a reference. Therefore, it's wise to make it clear to the potential employee that employment is dependent on receipt of a satisfactory reference from a former employer.[2]

CONTRACTS OF EMPLOYMENT AND THE LAW

As of November 1993, the Trade Union and Employment Rights Act 1993 (TURERA) requires that every employee who works more than eight hours each week must have a contract of employment issued to them within two months of their starting date.

The contract must contain specific items of information, and these are shown in the following checklist.

Contract of employment information checklist[3]

- name of the employer and the employee
- start date
- commencement of continuous service
- the scale or rate of remuneration; or the method of calculating remuneration
- the intervals at which remuneration is paid, e.g. weekly, monthly
- hours of work and normal working hours
- entitlement to holidays, including public holidays
- entitlement to holiday pay, including entitlement to accrued holiday pay on terminating employment
- provision of sick-pay, if any
- pensions and pension schemes
- the length of notice which the employee is obliged to give and the length of notice the employee is entitled to receive to terminate the contract of employment
- the title of the job which the employee is employed to do
- the disciplinary rules which apply to the employee

Discrimination

RACE RELATIONS ACT 1976

Discrimination whether:

- direct
- indirect
- victimization

is unlawful on the grounds of race, ethnic or national origins.

Direct discrimination involves treating someone less favourably because of their race or origins, e.g. 'We wouldn't want to appoint an Asian to the post of Finance Director'.

Indirect discrimination involves imposing a requirement or condition which, in practice, discriminates against particular minorities, e.g. organizing training courses on Friday nights and Saturdays, which would be totally unacceptable to an orthodox observer of the Jewish faith.

Victimization involves treating someone less favourably because they are, or have been, involved in proceedings in connection with the Race Relations Act.

SEX DISCRIMINATION ACT 1975 AND 1986

It is unlawful to discriminate, either directly or indirectly, or to victimize on grounds of sex or marital status, except where a particular sex or marital status could be shown to be a bona fide requirement.

An organization which, say, specified that all applicants must be 6' 1" (1.85 m) or over could well be accused of indirect discrimination because there are many more men of this height than there are women.

REHABILITATION OF OFFENDERS ACT 1974

Once a conviction has been 'spent', an organization cannot refuse to employ, promote, dismiss or otherwise discriminate against an ex-offender on the grounds that the ex-offender has a previous conviction. (See also p. 83.)

TRADE UNION REFORM AND EMPLOYMENT RIGHTS ACT 1993

(This Act amends Employment Protection (Consolidation) Act 1978.) Employees generally have the right to have no action taken against them as a penalty for joining, belonging to, or taking part in, the activities of an independent Trade Union. In practice, this means that an employer should not overlook an employee for promotion or advancement because the employee is, in some way, involved in trade union activities.

Disability

DISABLED PERSONS (EMPLOYMENT) ACT 1944 AND THE CHRONICALLY SICK AND DISABLED PERSONS ACT 1970

Organizations employing more than twenty people are required to ensure that 3 per cent of the workforce are registered as disabled.

DISABILITY DISCRIMINATION ACT 1995

This Act requires employers to make reasonable adjustments to both working practices and the working environment to overcome practical barriers to the employment of disabled people.[4]

Redundancy and the law

- Any company which is planning to make ten or more people redundant at one establishment over a period of thirty days or less, must give at least thirty days notice to staff, the trade union(s), and the Department of Employment
- Any company which is planning to make 100 or more people redundant at one establishment over a period of ninety days, must give at least ninety days notice to staff, the trade union(s), and the Department of Employment
- Calculations of redundancy payments depend on a number of factors including length of service, weekly pay and age. For example:
  - Darren is twenty-nine, has been with the company for six years, and is entitled to six weeks' statutory redundancy pay
  - Josie is fifty-three, has been with the company for six years, and is entitled to nine weeks' statutory redundancy pay

Booklet PL 808 (REV 3), 'Redundancy Payments' is obtainable free of charge from Department of Trade and Industry, Redundancy Payments Service, Hagley House, 83–85 Hagley Road, Edgbaston, Birmingham B16 8QG; Tel.: 0121 456 4411; Fax: 0121 454 9516.

The DTI also operate a helpline service which companies in England, Scotland and Wales can access free of charge. The telephone number is 0800 848 489.

Health and safety and the law

The laws and regulations which form the basis for UK health and safety are:

HEALTH AND SAFETY AT WORK ETC. ACT 1974

This piece of legislation sets out the general duties which employers have towards employees and members of the public, and which employees have to themselves and to each other. (See Section 4 for more information.)

THE MANAGEMENT OF HEALTH & SAFETY AT WORK REGULATIONS 1992

These regulations require employers to:

- carry out regular inspections to assess possible risk areas (at least every six months, more often in places where there are recognized hazards)
- inform employees, where appropriate, that they are working in risk areas
- take appropriate action to minimise risks
- provide employees with appropriate protection against the possible risk (protective clothing and equipment)
- inform employees of the person or people specifically nominated to oversee the risk

WORKPLACE (HEALTH, SAFETY & WELFARE) REGULATIONS 1992

These give the requirements relating to:

- maintenance of workplace, and of equipment, devices and systems
- ventilation
- temperature in indoor workplaces
- lighting
- cleanliness and waste materials
- room dimensions and space
- workstations and seating
- conditions of floors and traffic routes
- falls or falling objects
- windows and transparent or translucent doors, gates and walls
- windows, skylights and ventilators
- ability to clean windows etc. safely
- organization etc. of traffic routes
- doors and gates
- escalators and moving walkways

- sanitary conveniences
- washing facilities
- drinking water
- accommodation for clothing
- facilities for changing clothes
- facilities for rest and to eat meals

The *Approved Code of Practice: Workplace (Health, Safety & Welfare) Regulations 1992*, published by the HSE (ISBN 0 11 886333 9, £5.00) gives the new requirements in detail.

HEALTH AND SAFETY (DISPLAY SCREEN EQUIPMENT) REGULATIONS 1992

These set out the requirements regarding working with Visual Display Units (VDUs). *VDUs: an easy guide to the regulations* is published by the HSE (ISBN 0 7176 0735 6, £5.00).

PERSONAL PROTECTIVE EQUIPMENT (PPE) REGULATIONS 1992

These cover the law relating to the provision of protective clothing and equipment.

PROVISION AND USE OF WORK EQUIPMENT REGULATIONS (PUWER) 1992

These cover machinery and equipment provided by employers for use at work.

MANUAL HANDLING OPERATIONS REGULATIONS 1992

These cover the moving of objects by hand or bodily force.

The previous six Regulations, all of which came into force in January 1993, are often collectively referred to as the 'six-pack'.

HEALTH & SAFETY (FIRST AID) REGULATIONS 1981

These cover the provision of first aid in the workplace.

NOISE AT WORK REGULATIONS (1989)

These deal with the actions employers must take to protect employees from hearing damage.

ELECTRICITY AT WORK REGULATIONS (1989)

These cover the requirements relating to the safety and maintenance of electrical systems.

REPORTING OF INJURIES, DISEASES AND DANGEROUS OCCURRENCES REGULATIONS 1995 (RIDDOR)

(This is the revised version of the 1985 Regulations, and came into effect on 1 April 1996.) These cover employers' and managers' duties regarding the reporting of accidents etc. at work. A copy of the new 1995 Regulations can be obtained from the Health and Safety Executive special request telephone line on 0345 125499.

CONTROL OF SUBSTANCES HAZARDOUS TO HEALTH (COSHH) REGULATIONS 1988

These cover the use, storage and transportation of dangerous substances.

INDUSTRY SPECIFIC REGULATIONS

There is also a wide range of industry specific regulations. Although there are too many to list here, some examples are:

■ Chemicals (Hazard Information and Packaging for Supply) Regulations (CHIP 2) 1994, which suppliers must comply with when classifying, labelling and packing chemicals

■ Construction (Design and Management) Regulations 1994, with which employers and workers on construction sites must comply

■ Gas Safety (Installation and Use) Regulations 1994, which specify the safety regulations covering installation, maintenance and use of gas systems and appliances in domestic and commercial premises

■ Pressure Systems & Transportable Gas Containers Regulations 1989, which must be complied with by firms using pressure systems or gas containers

■ Supply of Machinery Safety Regulations, for firms supplying machinery and equipment

■ Woodworking Machines Regulations 1974, with which companies who process timber must comply

If you suspect that your organization needs to comply with industry specific regulations, contact the HSE General Enquiry line on 0541 545500.

Use the next activity as an opportunity to create a list of the health and safety publications you need to obtain.

ACTIVITY 28

Complete the chart below with the names of the health and safety publications, rules, regulations and legislation you need to obtain. Where possible, note down from where this information might be purchased or borrowed.

Health and safety information	Location

FEEDBACK

If you need information about Health & Safety Executive publications contact HSE Information Centre, Broad Lane, Sheffield S3 7HQ; Tel.: 0541 545500.

If you want to order Health & Safety Executive publications contact HSE Books, PO Box 1999, Sudbury, Suffolk CO10 6FS; Tel.: 01787 881165; Fax: 01787 313995.

Notes

1 Information in this section adapted from 'Law at Work' by Judith Howlings, *Personnel Management,* 30 May 1996.

2 Ibid.

3 Adapted from *A Handbook of Personnel Management Practice* by Michael Armstrong, Kogan Page, 4th edition (1994), p. 786.

4 *IPD Newsletter*, June 1996.

Summary

Now that you have completed the eleventh workbook in this series, you should feel confident about your ability to:

- recruit and select staff
- undertake disciplinary proceedings and conduct grievance interviews
- inform staff about proposed redundancies
- initiate counselling to tackle poor work performance
- plan, implement and monitor health and safety procedures
- recognize the law which applies to personnel and health and safety matters

In Workbook 3, *Understanding Business Process Management*, we will be examining the importance of quality assurance and looking at ways in which you can establish appropriate systems to improve and monitor processes within your organization.

Topics which have been touched upon in this workbook are covered in greater depth in later books in this series:

- Workbook 12: *Developing Yourself and Your Staff*
- Workbook 13: *Building a High Performance Team*
- Workbook 14: *The New Model Leader*
- Workbook 16: *Communication*

Recommended reading

Handbook of Personnel Management Practice, Michael Armstrong, Kogan Page, 4th edition (1994) (first published 1977)

Managing an Effective Operation, Eddie Fowler and Paul Graves, Butterworth-Heinemann/Institute of Management (1995)

The Manager's Guide to Solving Personnel Issues, Isobel Emanuel, Pitman Publishing/Institute of Management; (1994)

Redundancy Payments, Department of Trade & Industry, PL 808 (REV 3)

About the Institute of Management

The mission of the Institute of Management (IM) is to promote the development, exercise and recognition of professional management.

The IM is the leading professional organization for managers. Its efforts and resources are devoted to ensuring the continuing development and success of its members.

At the forefront of management standards, the IM provides a range of services for its members. These include flexible training programmes and a unique range of support services such as career counselling, enquiry and research facilities and preferential prices on IM publications and other IM products.

Further details about the Institute of Management may be obtained from:

Institute of Management
Management House
Cottingham Road
Corby
Northants
NN17 1TT

Telephone 01536 204222

We need your views

We really need your views in order to make the Institue of Management Open Learning Programme an even better learning tool for you. Please take time out to complete and return this questionnaire to Tessa Gingell, Pergamon Open Learning, Linacre House, Jordan Hill, Oxford OX2 8DP.

Name:..

Address:...

....

Title of workbook:..

If applicable, please state which qualification you are studying for. If not, please describe what study you are undertaking, and with which organization or college:

....

Please grade the following out of 10 (10 being extremely good, 0 being extremely poor):

Content: ....   Suitability for ability level: ....

Readability: ....   Qualification coverage: ....

What did you particularly like about this workbook?

....

Are there any features you disliked about this workbook? Please identify them.

....

Are there any errors we have missed?
If so, please state page number: ....

How are you using the material? For example, as an open learning course, as a reference resource, as a training resource, etc.

....

How did you hear about the Institue of Management Open Learning Programme?:

Word of mouth: Through my tutor/trainer: Mailshot:

Other (please give details):...

Many thanks for your help in returning this form.

Institute of Management
Open Learning Programme

This programme comprises seventeen workbooks, each on a core management topic with the latest management thinking, as well as a *User Guide* and a *Mentor Guide*.

Designed for self study through open learning, the workbooks cover all management experience from team building to budgeting, from the skills of self management to manage strategically for organizational success.

TITLE	*ISBN*	*Price*
The Influential Manager	0 7506 3662 9	£22.50
Managing Yourself	0 7506 3661 0	£22.50
Getting the Right People to Do the Right Job	0 7506 3660 2	£22.50
Understanding Business Process Management	0 7506 3659 9	£22.50
Customer Focus	0 7506 3663 7	£22.50
Getting TQM to Work	0 7506 3664 5	£22.50
Leading from the Front	0 7506 3665 3	£22.50
Improving Your Organization's Success	0 7506 3666 1	£22.50
Project Management	0 7506 3667 X	£22.50
Budgeting and Financial Control	0 7506 3668 8	£22.50
Effective Financial and Resource Management	0 7506 3669 6	£22.50
Developing Yourself and Your Staff	0 7506 3670 X	£22.50
Building a High Performance Team	0 7506 3671 8	£22.50
The New Model Leader	0 7506 3672 6	£22.50
Making Rational Decisions	0 7506 3673 4	£22.50
Communication	0 7506 3674 2	£22.50
Successful Information Management	0 7506 3675 0	£22.50
User Guide	0 7506 3676 9	£22.50
Mentor Guide	0 7506 3677 7	£22.50
Full set of workbooks plus *Mentor Guide* and *User Guide*	0 7506 3359 X	£370.00

To order: *(Please quote ISBNs when ordering)*

- College Orders: 01865 314333
- Account holders: 01865 314301
- Individual Purchases: 01865 314627

   (Please have credit card details ready)

For further information or to request a full series brochure, please contact:

Tessa Gingell on 01865 314477